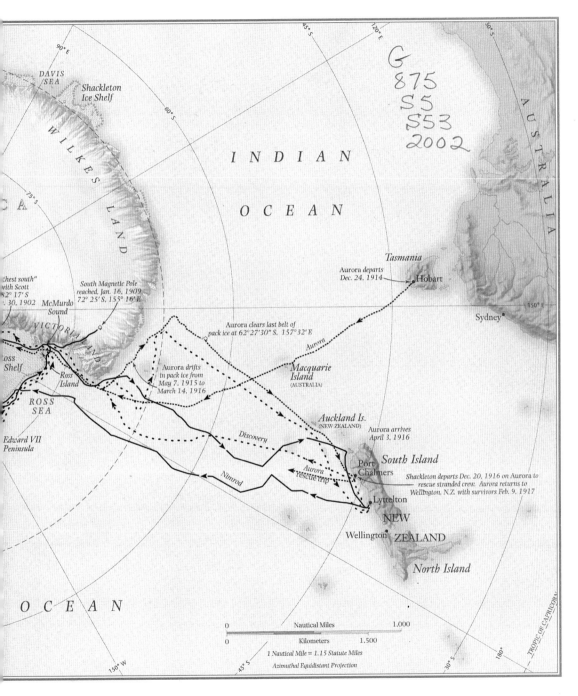

Shackleton

An Irishman in Antarctica

Shackleton

An Irishman in Antarctica

JONATHAN SHACKLETON

AND JOHN MacKENNA

THE UNIVERSITY OF WISCONSIN PRESS

To Daphne, David, Jane and Hannah
for their support

For Eoin O'Flaithearta

The University of Wisconsin Press
1930 Monroe Street
Madison, Wisconsin 53711

www.wisc.edu/wisconsinpress/

First published 2002 by
THE LILLIPUT PRESS LTD
62-63 Sitric Road, Arbour Hill, Dublin 7, Ireland.

A CIP record is available from the Library of Congress.

ISBN 0 299 18620 2

Designed and typeset in Sabon by Anú Design, Tara
Printed in Dublin by βetaprint

Contents

◆

Shackleton

An Irishman in Antarctica

SHACKLETON FAMILY TREE

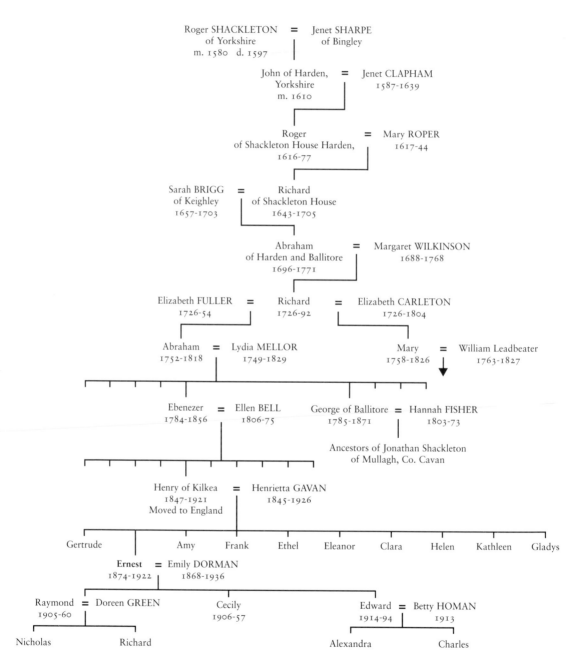

1

Irish Family Background

◆

The man was standing at the foot of the long incline, watching seven figures on the horizon. The first was moving carefully, the other six fanning out behind across the white country-side. The group travelled in a line, edging down the side of the slope, bent low against the sun. Gradually, the last of the seven began to lose contact with the others, his pace slowing, dropping farther and farther behind, until, finally, he came to a halt and crouched in the blinding whiteness. The others went on, too intent on their own expedition to notice his loss. Only when they had reached the security of level ground at the foot of the hill did they stop to take stock. The leading figure, by far the tallest of the seven, glanced back along the track they had descended and saw the distant figure, all but lost in the whiteness of the landscape.

'Mr Lag!'

There was no response from the distant figure.

'Mr Lag!'

The voice was louder now.

The crouching figure looked up, disorientated and surprised at how far he had fallen behind his comrades. Rising slowly and taking his bearings, he trudged down the hill, the snow-white heads of cow parsley hanging across his path.

'We can't wait all day for you, kindly keep up with the rest.'

*Kilkea House.
Built in the early
nineteenth century
for the Duke of
Leinster. Leased
by Ernest's father
Henry Shackleton
c.1872-80; six
of of his children
were born there.*

'Yes.'

'Now, on we go. Gertrude, you walk behind Ernest. That way we may keep from losing your brother. Again.'

And so the procession continued across the foot of Mullaghcreelan Hill. The nurse leading her charges through the long summer grasses, Amy and Frank and Ethel and Ernest and Gertrude Shackleton following in her footsteps.

The watching figure, Henry Shackleton, the children's father, turned back to examine his beloved roses, smiling at the picture of his eldest son, lost among the wild flowers, living in a world of his own.

The Shackleton children making that afternoon journey across the fields near Kilkea, in the south of Co. Kildare, were the descendants, on the one hand, of a family whose roots ran back to Quaker stock and who had arrived in the area two and a half centuries earlier. On the other, the family tree was grounded in the Fitzmaurices, a wild and adventurous Kerry family.

The Quakers, or Religious Society of Friends as they were more formally known, were founded by George Fox in the north of England in the mid-seventeenth century. The sect, like other similar groups of the time, was intent on moving away from the structured forms of the Church of England and the Catholic Church. William Edmundson had brought the ideals of the Quakers to Ireland, establishing the first Irish Quaker meeting in Lurgan in 1654.

What marked the early Quakers out from the plethora of other sects of their time was their belief in the Inward Light, a phrase they used for the direct link they believed themselves to have to the Holy Spirit. Not for them the notion of a clerical hierarchy of middlemen through whom God might be reached.

The Quakers, who earned their colloquial name from the custom of members quaking during meetings, were non-violent in creed and practice and brought a stringency of clothing, lifestyle and business to their daily lives.

Women and men were treated equally within their fellowship, and indeed women were among the earliest preachers of Quakerism in Ireland, though by 1700 their preaching was being discouraged by the Elders and their position eroded by the late seventeenth century influx of soldiery into the ranks of Irish Quakerism.

Not surprisingly, the Quakers in Ireland were to live paradoxical lives. Not only did they bring a new religious belief and practice into the country, they also laid the foundations for the development of a trader class that was, on the one hand, distinct from the Anglo-Irish Protestant landlords and, on the other, separate from the Irish Catholic peasant class. The more prominent early Irish Friends became known outside their own community through their involvement in business, and among the better known family names were Bewley, Jacob, Shackleton and Lamb. While both Protestant and Catholic ranks may have been envious of the newly emerging merchant group, their envy was tempered by the lack of ostentation shown by the Quakers. They had no desire to clamber into the world of the big house, nor to proselytize among their poorer Catholic neighbours.

Despite the attempts of the early Quakers to live quiet lives, they didn't always escape the often unwelcome attentions of their fellow citizens. Their dress, religious beliefs and refusal to swear oaths, use the names of days and months or the pronoun 'you' or even to have images on their chinaware, made them easy targets for vilification.

One of the earliest Quaker settlements in Ireland was at Ballitore in Co. Kildare, thirty miles south-west of Dublin. The first Quakers to arrive in the village had been John Barcroft and Abel Strettel, who bought lands there in the 1690s. They arrived into an already established but poverty-ridden community. The local land was poor and poorly cared for. Barcroft and Strettel set about changing that, planting trees, orchards and hedges, putting their own kind of order on the wilder landscape that had met them on arrival.

In 1708 a Meeting House was completed in the village, with others built in the nearby towns of Carlow in 1716 and Athy in 1780 (although the first Quaker meeting here was held in 1671).

Shackleton House, Harden, Yorkshire. The family owned the Harden property since the sixteenth century. The house was demolished in 1892, when the door and lintel stone were brought by the Shackletons to Lucan, County Dublin, and in 1983 given to the restored Quaker Meeting House in Ballitore, County Kildare.

While most early Quakers in Ballitore made their living from industry and farming, Abraham Shackleton chose to open a boarding school in the village in 1726, beginning the Shackleton connection with Quaker life in the area.

The Shackletons came from the village of Harden in West Yorkshire, England, and Abraham had been born in 1696. The studious youngster had lost both parents before his eighth birthday but he showed a tenacity that was to stand to him in establishing his school.

As a young man he became an assistant teacher in Skipton where he met his wife, Margaret Wilkinson. He came to Ireland as a tutor to the Quaker Cooper and Duckett families, who lived at Coopershill, near Carlow, and at Duckett's Grove, on the border of counties Carlow and Kildare, less than ten miles from Ballitore. Encouraged by these two families, Abraham established his school.

The initial roll for the school numbered thirty-eight pupils. Two years later the numbers had grown to sixty-three. The school became so successful in such a short time that its reputation drew students from as far afield as France, Norway and Jamaica. Many children, arriving in Ballitore at the age of four, were to remain there without seeing their parents again until they were eighteen. Some of the boys, falling prey to measles or smallpox, were never to return home, dying in the village to which they had come to be educated, far removed from parents and family. These tragedies, when they occurred through the years, cast shadows over Ballitore where everybody knew everybody else and many pupils lodged in local houses, integrating fully into village family life.

The curriculum in Ballitore School included the classics, history, maths, geography, English literature and writing and composition. Not all the teachers or pupils came from Quaker backgrounds and among early alumni were the statesman Edmund Burke (1729-97), the revolutionary Napper Tandy (1737-1803) and the future Cardinal Cullen (1803-78).

Above: Richard Shackleton (1726-1792) who succeeded his father as master of Ballitore School in 1756 until 1779, was a founding member of the Trinity College Debating Society, and a lifelong friend of Edmund Burke. (Courtesy Desna Greenhow)

Left: Abraham and Richard Shackleton. Abraham (1696 - 1771), born Harden, Yorkshire, where his father was the first of the family to be a Quaker, came to Ireland in 1720 and opened a school in Ballitore, County Kildare in 1726.

Shackleton School, Ballitore. Opened on the first of the third month 1726 by Abraham Shackleton and closed in 1836, having had over a thousand pupils. Building demolished c.1940.

When Richard Shackleton, Abraham's son, born in 1726, took over the running of the school thirty years later, he broadened the curriculum while introducing a more stringent regime, leaving little room for amusement. (His stringency led, on at least one occasion, in 1769, to the pupils locking the staff out of the school, demanding a summer holiday. Pacifist or not, the headmaster quickly broke down the school door and the boys were thrashed.) Richard had been a schoolmate and friend of Edmund Burke's in Ballitore and an observer of their student days commented that Shackleton was 'steadier and more settled than Burke was ever to become'.

Richard had received his first and second level education in Ballitore and had gone on to study languages at Trinity College in Dublin, the first Quaker to do so. He was an active member of the Historical Society and received a special dispensation to address the Society while wearing his hat – a Quaker practice based on the belief that all people were equal and none in particular merited the doffing of a hat. The attractions of *the world* might have drawn another young man away from Ballitore and Quakerism but not Richard. He was single-minded in his commitment to his faith and his education.

Eighteenth-century Quakers were forbidden from taking degrees so Richard, having completed his studies in Trinity, returned to the quieter and more austere life of a school-master in Ballitore.

At the age of twenty-three he married Elizabeth Fuller, a granddaughter of John Barcroft, one of the original settlers at Ballitore. The couple had four children. Elizabeth died in 1754 and a year later Richard married Sarah Carleton. They had two surviving children – Elizabeth and Mary.

Mary was to leave a legacy of history, culture and literature through her poetry and prose. Richard had insisted his daughters receive as wide an education as his sons and in Mary's case he greatly encouraged her in her writing. When he travelled abroad, to London and Yorkshire, Mary travelled with him. While visiting cousins in Selby in Yorkshire, they were invited to tea in house after house. Typically, Mary noted in her diaries that the silver coffee-pot from the local big house was there to greet them on each tea-table in turn.

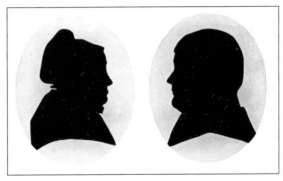

Mary and William Leadbeater. Mary (1758-1826), daughter of Richard Shackleton and his second wife Elizabeth, was a prolific poet, correspondent and diarist. William (1763-1827), Mary's husband, an orphan, attended Ballitore School. Their daughter Lydia Fisher was a secret love of Limerick-born novelist Gerald Griffin (1803-40). Plain silhouettes were the usual form of portrait for Quakers.

Born in 1758, Mary had developed both an academic and a personal friendship with the other pupils in Ballitore School. One of her close school friends, William Leadbeater, was to return to Ballitore as a teacher and, at the age of thirty-three, Mary married him. All the while, Ballitore School was growing in size – as many as twenty-three new pupils enrolling in one year.

Richard Shackleton died of a sudden fever in 1792, on his way to a school board meeting in the town of Mountmellick. He was sixty-six. The running of the school was now taken over by his eldest son Abraham.

Abraham was to undo many of the changes his father had made. Where Richard had widened the curriculum, Abraham narrowed its focus. Where Richard had thrown open the school doors to a multitude of denominations, Abraham restricted entry to Quakers.

As the eighteenth century drew to a close, Abraham married Lydia Mellor and set about tracing the family history, bringing to light, among other things, the family crest and motto, *Fortitudine Vincimus – By Endurance We Conquer.*

Whether the changes introduced by Abraham would have led to the decline that followed in Ballitore School is impossible to tell, but the rebellion of 1798 brought an immediate dip in its fortunes. That the rebellion should occur in that year was hardly surprising.

Ireland in the 1790s was a country riven with dissension. It had a parliament established for its minority community, while its Catholic population was petitioning for King and Parliament to 'relieve them from their degraded situation and no longer suffer them to continue like strangers in their native land'.

In April 1790 a meeting was held in Belfast where those attending agreed to 'form ourselves into an association to unite all Irishmen to pledge themselves to our country'. Thus was the foundation laid for the founding of the revolutionary United Irishmen, whose first Secretary was Napper Tandy, former pupil of Ballitore. Through the 1790s the United Irishmen worked to establish their organization across the country. They drew inspiration and aid from revolutionary France and their ambition was a rebellion that would overthrow British dominance in Ireland and establish an independent state, unifying Catholic, Protestant and Dissenter against the imposition of rule, through a puppet parliament, from Britain. As the power of the United Irishmen grew, Parliamentary Acts were introduced in 1794 to outlaw their meetings, but the organization continued, underground, as a secret society. The following year a Catholic Relief Bill, designed to make daily life easier for the vast majority of the population, was defeated in Parliament.

Nor were the United Irishmen the only ones with an interest in Ireland's political future. In 1779 the first regular Volunteer Corps was founded in Belfast. The immediate objective of the Volunteers was to defend Ireland, in the absence of sufficient British troops, against invasion by French or American marauders. The incident, which sparked panic among the citizenry, was the capture of a ship in Belfast Lough by American privateer Captain Paul Jones.

Mary Leadbeater's house, Ballitore. From here Mary recorded many of the comings and goings in the village. Building recently restored and open to the public. (Photograph c.1890s)

Initially, the Volunteers were Protestant but they were armed, and an armed group of citizens was a frightening prospect for the government. And worse, as the Volunteers spread, Catholics were welcomed into their ranks and an organization that had started as a last line of defence quickly became a potential threat.

The drain of British soldiery from Ireland reached crisis point in the 1790s because of war with France. England's problem was seen, by the United Irishmen, as their opportunity to push for a full rebellion and by those loyal to the Crown as a chance to establish a Yeomanry force within the country.

Arrests of suspected United Irishmen continued through 1796 and 1797. In October of that year *habeas corpus* was suspended to deal with trouble from both the United Irishmen and the emerging loyalist Orange Order.

Early in 1798 the United Irishmen in Leinster resolved that they 'would not be diverted from their purpose by anything which could be done in parliament'. In May a rebellion organized by the United Irishmen broke out in many Leinster counties, including Kildare. Ballitore did not escape the bloodshed.

Parents, fearing for their children's welfare, in a village where violence, warfare and murder had become commonplace, removed them as quickly as possible. Despite the fall in numbers, the school struggled on until in 1801 Abraham decided to close it.

Several years earlier William Leadbeater had left teaching and gone into business and Mary had opened the first Post Office in Ballitore. This allowed her to continue her writing and kept her well informed about local comings and goings.

While her main concern was with local life, Mary also corresponded widely with people like Edmund Burke and the novelist Maria Edgeworth (1767-1849), as well as a wide circle of past pupils across the globe. While Burke had been an acquaintance at school, Maria Edgeworth became an epistolary friend. Their letters grew out of a shared interest in the improvement of the peasantry and in the education of women, a topic Edgeworth had used for her first publication, *Letters to Literary Ladies*, published in 1796.

It is Mary's insatiable appetite for gossip that makes her diaries so interesting. They were published long after her death as *The Annals of Ballitore* (1862), generally called *The Leadbeater Papers*, and deal with the period 1766 to 1824. They include one of the few impartial accounts of the 1798 rebellion, which began on 23 May and continued with sporadic fighting until mid-July.

At the end of 1798 Mary noted the constant presence of the reminders of loss in her own and others' lives.

'*Late one evening, as we leaned over the bridge, we saw a gentleman and a lady watering their horses at the river, attended by servants fully armed. They wore mourning habits, and though young and newly married, looked very serious and sorrowful. Their chastened appearance, their armed servants, the stillness of the air scarcely broken by a sound, rendered the scene very impressive ... Mourning was the language – mourning was the dress of the country.*'

Mary was also deeply involved in the movement to 'improve' the peasantry and to promote ideals of progress, abstinence, thrift and self-esteem. These were the principles evinced by her

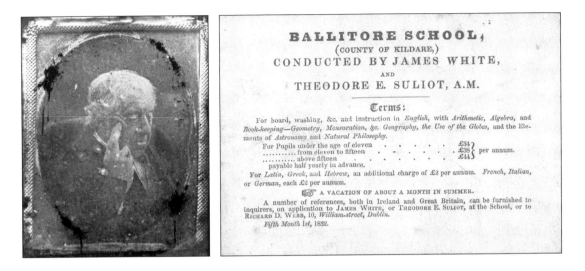

BALLITORE SCHOOL,
(COUNTY OF KILDARE,)
CONDUCTED BY JAMES WHITE,
AND
THEODORE E. SULIOT, A.M.

Terms:

For board, washing, &c. and instruction in *English*, with *Arithmetic, Algebra,* and *Book-keeping—Geometry, Mensuration, &c. Geography, the Use of the Globes,* and the Elements of *Astronomy* and *Natural Philosophy.*

For Pupils under the age of eleven . . . . . £34⎫
.... from eleven to fifteen . - . . . . £38⎬ per annum.
.... above fifteen . . . . . . £44⎭
payable half yearly in advance.

For *Latin, Greek,* and *Hebrew,* an additional charge of £2 per annum. *French, Italian,* or *German,* each £2 per annum.

☞ A VACATION OF ABOUT A MONTH IN SUMMER.

A number of references, both in Ireland and Great Britain, can be furnished to inquirers, on application to JAMES WHITE, or THEODORE E. SULIOT, at the School, or to RICHARD D. WEBB, 10, *William-street, Dublin.*

Fifth Month 1st, 1832.

grandfather and father through Ballitore School, and she was anxious that they become part of the lives of those about her.

In 1806, five years after the school had closed its doors, Abraham Shackleton's son-in-law James White reopened them and with the return of peace to the countryside the classrooms quickly filled with students from Ireland and elsewhere.

Abraham, however, decided not to become reinvolved and turned, instead, to milling as a second profession, running the family mill at Ballitore and continuing to work there until his death in 1818.

Milling carried through to the next generation with Abraham and Lydia's son Ebenezer, who bought a mill in the village of Moone, a couple of miles along the road from Ballitore.

Ebenezer, born in 1784, had grown up in a Quaker family but from early adulthood questioned the direction Quakerism was taking in Ireland, believing the community was straying from its original ideals. He took this as his main reason for converting to the Church of Ireland and bringing his children up in that faith. One of those children was Henry Shackleton, father of the young walkers spread out across the sunlit fields on Mullaghcreelan Hill.

Left: James White (1778-1847), master at Ballitore School (1806-36), married the previous master Abraham Shackleton's daughter Lydia. Their daughter Hannah married a teacher at the school, Theodore Suliot and they emigrated to Ohio. After Lydia's death White married Mary Pike. (Ambrotype courtesy Jeremy White)

Above: Terms of enrolment of school in 1832.

Ebenezer Shackleton (1784-1856), married secondly Ellen Bell, grandparents of EHS. Ebenezer took on the Moone Mill in 1824 and lived at Moone Cottage (now demolished). (Courtesy the late Betty Chinn)

On the other side of the family, the children's mother Henrietta was the daughter of John Henry Gavan and Caroline Mary Fitzmaurice. Henrietta's mother was the daughter of John Fitzmaurice of Carlow, himself the great-grandson of William Fitzmaurice, the twentieth Baron of Kerry.

The Fitzmaurices, through marriage into the Petty family, had inherited large tracts of the Petty estate of 270,000 acres in Kerry. (William Petty (1623-87) had been Cromwell's physician-general and surveyor.) But their roots in the area went back much further, to Thomas Fitzmaurice who had arrived as part of the Norman force in Ireland in the thirteenth century. Fitzmaurice had been styled the First Lord of Kerry. The earldoms of Kerry and Shelbourne and the title of Marquess of Lansdowne were subsequently created for members of the Fitzmaurice family.

Not that the Fitzmaurices had escaped political and military troubles in the course of Irish history. In the Geraldine rebellion of 1579 the family had much of their lands seized and sold.

In July that year James Fitzmaurice had landed at Smerwick harbour in Co. Kerry and established a base at Dún an Oir with a force of Spanish and Italian soldiers. The Papal Legate, Nicholas Sanders, accompanied him, with letters from the Pope to the Irish Lords discharging them from allegiance to Queen Elizabeth of England and urging them to rebel in support of the Catholic faith. Two months later Fizmaurice was killed in a skirmish with the Burke clan in Co. Limerick.

In 1691 lands were again confiscated when James and Henry Fitzmaurice remained loyal to King James against King William. Later, the family returned to the safer confines of the establishment. The First Marquess was First Secretary and then Prime Minister in Britain from 1782 to 1783. The Third Marquess was Chancellor of the Exchequer from 1806 to 1807 and later Home Secretary. The Fifth Marquess was Viceroy of India from 1888 to 1894 and subsequently British Foreign Secretary.

On the Gavan side, Henrietta was descended from a family connected to church and state. Her father, Henry, had been involved, with his father Rev. John Gavan, rector of Wallstown, Doneraile, Co. Cork, in the battle of Wallstown, a tithe-assessing incident (whereby a tenth of annual produce was levied in support of the Anglican Church) which occurred in September 1832.

Rev. John Gavan was an unpopular man in the area. He and his son had gone, one afternoon, to mark tithes on a farm. Once there, an angry crowd surrounded them. The Gavans drew their pistols but were disarmed. The following day, with three magistrates and a number of policemen, they went to another farm. Some stoning of the police and magistrates, mostly by women and children, followed and, apparently, one of the magistrates, a man called Evans, panicked and ordered the soldiers to open fire on the crowd. Four of the tenants were killed, one a boy of fourteen, and many were injured.

A subsequent investigation suggested that the turning points that led to the heightening of tensions and the subsequent deaths were Henry Gavan's over-zealousness and Evans's panic.

Henry had originally studied medicine and qualified as a doctor but his interest lay in joining the Royal Irish Constabulary. Through the political influence of Lord Cornwallis, Henry obtained a commission in the RIC, and after his marriage in 1844, to Caroline Mary Fitzmaurice of Carlow, he was appointed Inspector General of Police in Ceylon.

Henry and Caroline sailed from Falmouth for Ceylon on the *Persia*. Shortly after its departure, the ship was forced to return to Falmouth after a ten day buffeting at sea. The Gavans refused to re-embark. Such was the ferocity of the experience, Henry never fully recovered and died two years later, leaving his wife and an infant daughter, Henrietta Letitia.

Henrietta's birth, on 28 September 1845, came just two weeks before the first reports of a widespread potato failure in Ireland. Over the following three years Ireland would go through the bleakest period of its history.

Failure of the staple diet crop of potatoes through 1845, '46, '47 and '48 was mirrored by trader speculation which saw the price of corn rise beyond the means of the destitute, and by government inaction. The relief measures introduced were often ill-conceived and badly organized.

Help did arrive from abroad, mainly from the United States, but distribution was haphazard. By 1848 more than a million people had died from starvation and malnutrition. Those who were healthy enough and could find the fare emigrated, leaving a devastated country.

For those who stayed, eviction was a constant threat. With crops continuing to fail and no money available for rents, the poorhouses and roadsides were thronged with evicted families. By 1 July 1848, almost 840,000 people were in receipt of relief.

The Great Famine, however, was not a matter of life and death for all classes in Ireland. Caroline Gavan had lost her husband but neither she nor her daughter was in any danger of falling victim to starvation or emigration. The effects of the famine did not impinge materially on the lifestyle of the Gavans or their class.

Brought up by her mother, Henrietta grew into a bright, vivacious and good-humoured young woman. On 28 February 1872 she married Henry Shackleton and moved with him to live at Kilkea House, a large square, comfortable farmhouse. To the side, as one entered, were solidly built, slated stone outhouses which enclosed a courtyard.

Everton, Crockaun, County Laois, a Fitzmaurice house outside Carlow from where EHS's parents were married. Kelvin Grove and Laurel Lodge were other Fitzmaurice houses in the Carlow area.

The house was surrounded by rolling grassland that rose along the flank of Mullaghcreelan Hill on one side, and fell to the banks of the river Griese on the other. It was rich land, good for tillage as well as cattle and sheep rearing.

Henrietta's verve and sheer good humour were to help her create – even in difficult times – a sense of order, enjoyment and support for her children at Kilkea.

Unusually in a Victorian family, both Henry and Henrietta were constantly available to their children, including them in virtually all family activities, listening and advising and, most of all, encouraging them to express themselves.

These two family lines – hardworking Quaker pacifists and hot-blooded adventurers – were to find a perfect point of fusion in Ernest.

Bent low between his rose bushes, Henry's thoughts had moved away from the sight of Ernest, lost in wonder among the cow parsley, to the more pressing business of money. He had hoped to make a living as a farmer and find time and opportunity to develop his interest in homoeopathy, but, confronted with falling prices and a downturn in the agricultural economy, he faced the possibility of a change of career. It wouldn't be his first.

Henry had been sent to school in Wellington College in England, carrying his mother's hopes of an army commission, but ill health had brought him back to Ireland and to Trinity College in Dublin, where he took an Arts degree in 1868.

Four years later, when he married Henrietta, they opted for a life of farming. Land was leased from the Duke of Leinster and the couple set up home at Kilkea House. The farm, set close to the hamlet of Kilkea – built to house workers on the estate of the Duke of Leinster – was equidistant from the market towns of Athy and Carlow and close to the village of Castledermot.

With family connections on both sides, they were five miles from Henry's birthplace and seven miles from Henrietta's mother's home in Carlow; there were numerous friends and relatives to visit in the area and they enjoyed the freedom that rural life allowed. Wandering the fields and the banks of the river Griese, which flowed through the farm, Henry could indulge his passion for collecting herbs. Henrietta travelled regularly to visit relatives in Carlow and the couple became part of the local social life.

Their time at Kilkea was to prove a fertile one, six of their ten children being born in the house over the following seven years. Their first, Gertrude, arrived at the end of 1872.

At five o'clock on the morning of 15 February 1874 Henrietta gave birth to the couple's second child, Ernest Henry. A year later Amy was born and a second son, Frank, was born in 1876. In 1878 the new arrival was Ethel and the last of the Kilkea children, Eleanor, was born in 1879.

With six children to raise, Henry and his wife had to face the fact that farming could no longer provide them with a livelihood.

While the famine days of the 1840s were past, there were still regular crop failures due to blight. More importantly, the whole question of land ownership and reform hung over the future of farming in Ireland, and the previous two decades witnessed the cumulative and spreading force of agrarian tension.

Land and its ownership had never been far removed from Irish politics, as the Gavan family would have known. By 1858 the introduction of the Landed Estates (Ireland) Act brought the question of land ownership and control back into the domestic limelight. The 1860 Land Improvements (Ireland) Act had made provision for loans to tenants for the erection of labourers' cottages but the issue of the ownership of land ran much deeper. The movement towards independence, which had grown out of the 1798 rebellion and the evictions following the Great Famine and led to the abortive Fenian rebellion of 1867, was inseparable from the land question.

The failure of the Fenian rising had done little to stem the tide of demands for reform and through the 1870s there were regular calls for action by the British government. In 1878 Michael Davitt – who would found the Land League in October 1879 – was demanding 'agrarian agitation'. His calls were met with support across the country and tenants were organising themselves in virtually every parish. This political uncertainty, coupled with a periodic downturn in agricultural prices, meant that farming looked less and less promising.

Henry was neither accountant nor politician and, despite the children's happiness at Kilkea, he and Henrietta concluded that they must move on and find an alternative way of making a living. Medicine seemed to offer the best hope.

The sound of the children's laughter caught Henry's attention and he stood to watch them troop across the yard. Again, Ernest was lagging behind, Mr Lag by nickname and Mr Lag by nature. And then, at the sound of passing carriages, the boy was gone, racing along the gravelled path, out through the gate and onto the lane that ran past the house. Henry hurried to follow his son.

'It's just a funeral, sir,' the nurse assured him.

Henry slowed his pace and walked to the gate where he stood watching Ernest. The young boy was trotting after the receding carriages, his short legs working to carry him closer to the hearse. At the end of the lane, where it met the main road between Castledermot and Athy, the funeral cortège picked up speed, leaving Ernest far behind. Only then did he stop running and turn again for home. His father smiled, seeing the boy idling slowly towards him, amused by his son's fascination with funerals.

Later, when the afternoon was at its hottest, Henry took the children swimming in the nearby river and they repeated the old family joke over and over, laughing boisterously, as they plunged into the clear water.

'You swim in the Griese and come out dripping!'

While Henry and Henrietta prepared to move to Dublin, life at Kilkea House continued as it had done. The children played in the garden, the scent of the climbing roses, which shadowed the walls of the house, blending with the perfume of the wild honeysuckle that threaded through the field hedges. Passing carts and carriages on the road between Athy and Castledermot drew them to the end of the field that fronted the house. This passing traffic and the occasional trips the family took to the surrounding towns broke the rhythm of their days at home.

On one such family visit, to their cousins at Browne's Hill in Carlow, Ernest saw, for the first time, a penguin skin. He was fascinated by the pelt, given as a gift to the Brownes. It was unlike anything he had ever seen. He was well used to the moth-eaten fox heads mounted on the walls of many of the houses he visited, and the stuffed remains of tigers and lions brought from India and Africa, while uncommon, were not extraordinary. But this penguin skin was different. Its shape and colour and texture intrigued the young boy and set his imagination racing. There were endless questions about its origins and its habitat. He conjured up stories about where it had come from and how it had reached his corner of the globe. It remained a source of curiosity for a long time and, on subsequent visits, it was the first thing he sought out in the house.

Henrietta Shackleton (1845-1926), née Gavan, married Henry 28 February 1872. (Athy Heritage Centre)

Henry Shackleton (1847-1921), fifth eldest son of Ebenezer and Ellen Shackleton's ten children, and father of EHS. His vigorous beard earned him the nickname 'Parnell' when he returned to Trinity College. Appropriately, he favoured Home Rule. (Athy Heritage Centre)

The last thing Ernest did at Kilkea House, before climbing into the carriage that would take him away from his birthplace, was to stand on the fallen tree trunk on the lawn. This had been his ship's cabin for as long as he could remember, the place where he played on summer afternoons and lay long into the evening, watching the stars appear over Mullaghcreelan Hill, singing his favourite song quietly to himself.

> *'Twinkle, twinkle, little star,*
> *how I wonder what you are,*
> *up above the world so high,*
> *like a diamond in the sky.'*

Only then did he join the others waiting to leave for a new life in Dublin, where his father would begin his medical studies in Trinity College.

The Shackleton family settled at 35 Marlborough Road in South Dublin and Ernest immediately requisitioned the garden frame as a replacement for the ship's cabin he had left behind on the lawn at Kilkea House. The house in Marlborough Road was a two-storey over basement, red-bricked dwelling, with gardens back and front, built a decade before the Shackletons moved there and part of the new development of lands close to the suburban village of Donnybrook.

Life in Dublin offered fresh wonders to be explored. For the children, St Stephen's Green, recently opened to

35 Marlborough Road, Dublin, home 1880-84 to Henry and Henrietta, their six children and three more daughters born there. A commemorative plaque was unveiled by EHS's granddaughter, Alexandra Shackleton, in May 2000.

the public, was a place of excursion with their nurse, while the newly opened manual telephone exchange in Dame Street, with its five subscribers, was a topic for comment and discussion over the dining table.

But for Ernest Marlborough Road provided another diversion. A regular procession of passing funerals meant he could more easily indulge his passion for playing chief mourner, watching for the cortèges from the front window and racing down the granite steps to follow the processions.

While Henry pursued medicine at Trinity, the family expanded with the arrival of Clara in 1881, Helen in 1882 and Kathleen in 1884. For Ernest, these additions were little more than distractions, as he had other undertakings to pursue.

The first was the excavation of a large hole in the back garden, which, he told his father, would eventually take him to Australia. The second involved borrowing one of his mother's rings. Having liberated it from her room he buried it in the garden and arranged for his nurse to be present when he unearthed the unexpected treasure, glorying in her surprise and delight.

Evenings were spent reading and sketching. Ernest had had some lessons in sketching and, even as a child, was keen to develop this talent. The Jules Verne stories in the *Boys'*

Aberdeen House, 12 West Hill (now Westwood Road), Sydenham, where the Shackletons moved in June 1885, when Henry started his practice as a local doctor for the next thirty-two years.

EHS aged eleven, when he was a pupil at Fir Lodge Preparatory School, Sydenham, London.

Own Paper were Ernest's favourite reading material. Indeed, as a quiet child, he often seemed most happy with his own company, not that solitary moments were frequent in a house where there were now nine children.

As at Kilkea, mealtimes regularly found the family playing a favourite game of *capping* quotations, with Henry giving the children a fragment which they would try to complete. Ernest was particularly adept at this, Tennyson being his favourite source.

In 1884 Henry qualified, with distinction, taking an M.B. and M.D. from Trinity College. Again, it was decision time. Henry and his wife discussed the possibilities of establishing a practice in Dublin but opted for the greater opportunities offered by London.

In December 1884 Henry, Henrietta and their nine children sailed on the *Banshee* from Kingstown (now Dun Laoghaire) across the Irish Sea to Holyhead, and travelled from there to London.

The Shackleton's first home in London was in South Croydon. Despite Henry's best attempts, he found it impossible to establish a successful practice there and, the year after his arrival in England, he moved the family to Aberdeen House, 12 West Hill (now Westwood Road) in Sydenham. Two years later, in January 1887, Henrietta gave birth to the couple's tenth child, Gladys.

Life as a doctor was more rewarding for Henry in Sydenham. Henrietta, however, worn out by the birth of ten children, fell victim to a mysterious illness which left her without any energy. It was a sickness that Henry might have come across in Kilkea, where the locals would have described it as *the mionaerach*, a disease that wouldn't kill but debilitates the sufferer with little or no energy. Henrietta, so long the vital and good-humoured heart of the family, withdrew to her sick-room and rarely left it until her death in September 1926.

Despite their mother's illness, the children set about establishing new lives for themselves and were enrolled in schools in Sydenham. Ernest began attending Fir Lodge Preparatory School and rapidly acquired a new nickname, Micky, which also stuck at home. His new schoolmates found his Irish accent and manner an easy target for their sarcastic jibes. He had arrived a quiet and pacific boy but in his early days at the school he obviously decided it was time for a change. As a result he quickly acquired the reputation of 'a brave little fellow, ready to fight the universe and all therein'.

Among the friends he made at school the closest was Maurice Sale-Barker. They played football together and mercilessly taunted the younger Shackleton sisters.

Meanwhile, Henry was busy establishing his medical practice. The difficulty of bringing up a large family, pursuing a career in medicine and looking after an ailing wife did nothing to dent his enthusiasm for work.

Among his patients was Eleanor Marx, daughter of Karl Marx. Eleanor lived just around the corner from the Shackletons, in Jew's Walk, and it was to her house that Henry was called one afternoon in March 1898. Arriving quickly, he found that, as a reaction to the end of a love affair, she had taken an overdose of prussic acid and died before he could be of any help.

However, most of Henry's cases were more mundane. He was a hardworking man, popular with his patients and as a result he built up a thriving practice which was to continue in Sydenham for thirty-two years.

In 1887 Ernest was enrolled at Dulwich College as a day-boarder. The college had been founded in 1618 and, while not in the first rank of public schools, had a substantial reputation for producing businessmen and civil servants, the backbone of the middle class. It drew its boys from the locality and from families that were solvent rather than wealthy. In later years it would become known as the *alma mater* of P.G. Wodehouse and Raymond Chandler.

While Ernest was extremely accomplished at boxing and gym, and did well at cricket and football, his academic achievements at Dulwich were marked by a succession of reports through which ran the common thread that he could apply himself more, work much harder and do a great deal better. John Quiller Rowett (later the main sponsor of Shackleton's final *Quest* expedition) used to walk with him to school and wrote: 'He was always full of life and jokes, but was never very fond of lessons ... I had a friend who knew German very well, and I used to get hints from him which I passed on to Shackleton.'

Boredom rather than lack of ability was Ernest's chief problem. He excelled at the things he enjoyed and went to great lengths to collect foreign stamps, for instance. But he found little in the way of inspiration in the droning of his masters.

However his interest in the sea and all things maritime was growing. He regularly spent schooldays playing truant with friends near the local railway line. There the boys would cook over an open fire, smoke endless cigarettes and listen to Ernest reading stories of sea-faring and adventure. Their campfire talk turned, time and again, to the exciting prospect of running away and joining a ship. Eventually, words led to action and the friends made the journey to London Bridge to enlist on a ship. They queued for an interview with the Chief Steward, who took one look at the motley crew and sent them packing.

Ernest wasn't in the slightest discouraged by this setback. The idea of a life before the mast grew and he never missed an opportunity to discuss it at home. The young Shackleton was insistent that he didn't want to continue in school and his obvious unhappiness was treated sympathetically. The openness and patience with which all of the children's problems had been entertained by their parents continued into their adolescence. While Ernest's father had hoped he might follow him into the medical profession, he never insisted on it as a career.

They promised, on condition his school performance improved, to try and get him onto a ship. The Royal Navy was ruled out. Money to put a son in the navy was simply not

available. Undaunted and encouraged by the possibility of escape, Ernest set his mind to his academic work and his school performance improved greatly.

Henry's cousin, Rev. G.W. Woosnam, a member of the Mersey Mission to Seamen, was called on for help, and he arranged for the boy to make a trial voyage on the *Hoghton Tower* out of Liverpool.

Easter 1890 brought freedom for Ernest as he said his farewell to Dulwich College, an institution to which he wouldn't return for nineteen years – as a lauded past-pupil presenting the school awards on prize-giving day.

Dulwich College., the secondary school in London attended by EHS as day pupil 1887-90 and by his brother Frank 1891-3. Home of the James Caird and venue for the biannual meetings of the James Caird Society.

31

2

Merchant Navy Years

1890–1901

◆

When Ernest Shackleton boarded the *Hoghton Tower* in Liverpool as a ship's boy on 30 April 1890, he was stepping back and stepping forward. Forward into a life on the high seas, backward onto a ship whose time had passed, a square rigger whose sails might be strikingly beautiful but whose demands were beyond anything experienced on the steamships that were changing the face of maritime history.

The Shackleton family might have harboured social aspirations in moving to London, but Ernest was well aware that in the Merchant Navy he was apprenticed into the poor man's Royal Navy.

Life on the *Hoghton Tower* was everything that life at home was not. The adoration of his sisters and the warm concern of his parents were replaced by the hardship of a life at sea, with men who had little regard for anything beyond the apprentice's ability to do his job.

Shackleton the teetotaller now came face to face with a life where alcohol was one of the few distractions available. His habit of quoting poetry was met with bemusement, though his fondness for reading his Bible proved more acceptable. 'The first night I took out my Bible to read,' he wrote to his parents, 'they all stopped talking and laughing, and now every one of them reads theirs excepting a Roman Catholic, and he reads his prayer book.'

Hoghton Tower, *a
fully rigged 1600-ton
clipper at Newcastle,
New South Wales,
Australia, in 1893
where they took on
coal. EHS was an
apprentice on this
trip, his third voyage.*

Shackleton's first days on the *Hoghton Tower* were blessed with calm seas and a fair wind although that didn't prevent his suffering seasickness. Having found his sea legs and with good weather, he must have imagined life had little better to offer, but change was coming and harsher realities were just over the horizon.

Shackleton's maiden voyage took him to Valparaiso in Chile. His first experience of Cape Horn, like that of many other sailors, was an unhappy one. The *Hoghton Tower* reached the Cape in severe weather. Mountainous waves and gale-force winds pounded boat and crew, spars were damaged and several sailors were injured. The gales continued to pursue the old ship round the Horn. Shackleton was to learn that weather at sea bore no resemblance to weather on dry land. Romantic notions were blown away.

33

'It is pretty hard work and dirty work,' he wrote. 'You carry your life in your hand whenever you go aloft, in bad weather; how would you like to be 150 feet up in the air, hanging on with one hand to a rope while with the other you try to get the sail in.'

Despite the demands of work and weather, the young Shackleton was fortunate in that Captain Partridge was a kind man who had the interest of his crew at heart. Occasionally, he invited the apprentice to dine at his table. The youngster, for his part, was impetuous, adventurous and stubborn, having little or no time for red tape – the characteristics that made him resolute about his work and popular with his shipmates.

Valparaiso proved a welcome haven after the trauma of rounding the Horn. From there the *Hoghton Tower* sailed up the Chilean coast to Iquique, a port on the edge of the Atacama Desert, where she spent six weeks loading nitrates. The work was tedious, the port depressing, and Shackleton was learning another lesson about the hardships of a life at sea. Danger, boredom and demanding work were three of the greatest tests the novice would face.

The *Hoghton Tower* returned via Hamburg and Shackleton reached home on 22 April 1891. Captain Partridge spoke with Archdeacon Woosnam about Shackleton on his return, describing him as 'the most pig-headed obstinate boy I have ever come across but no real fault is found with him'. Partridge's willingness to take him aboard again, however, showed that pig-headedness and obstinacy could be a virtue.

Shackleton was greeted like a prodigal son by his parents and sisters but his stay with them was short. Nine weeks after his arrival, he was gone once more, to begin his full apprenticeship. Again, he sailed on the *Hoghton Tower*, leaving Cardiff on 25 June bound for Iquique. There was one major difference in this trip, however. Robert Robinson, a tough, no-nonsense man who cracked a harsh disciplinary whip, had replaced Partridge.

Robinson's autocratic attitude didn't help in settling the young man but there were other pressures. His unhappiness was compounded by extreme homesickness. He knew what lay ahead – good and bad – and the nine weeks he had spent with his family had left a residue of warm feeling that was at odds with the authoritarian manner of the new captain. On top of all this, there were the demands of his apprenticeship. His first voyage had been one of discovery, this was one of judgment.

To take his mind off his homesickness, Shackleton worked hard. During his leisure periods he wrote long letters, urging his sisters to write back and inventing games for them to play.

His three younger sisters would recall that he always arranged that there be three prizes for these contests, so that none would feel left out. When he wasn't writing, working or studying, Shackleton spent much of his time reading. Sometimes the sober words of the Bible, sometimes the lighter passages of *Vanity Fair*.

All his life Shackleton valued friendships and family. On January 1892 he wrote to a schoolfriend from Iquique, 'I am anxiously looking out for a letter from you but I suppose you have forgotten my existence altogether. Being away is I suppose "out of sight out of mind".'

Whatever about the toughness of Captain Robinson, the second mate on the ship was far more encouraging to the apprentice, urging him on in his studies and helping him learn the ropes of sailing. This was all the young man needed and he responded with enthusiasm. He might not always agree with his superiors but he was prepared to dedicate himself to those who showed any sign of believing in him.

Cape Horn proved no more hospitable the second time round. There were storms, high seas and injuries. Shackleton was extremely sick from lumbago for much of the journey. Reaching Chile he endured a bout of dysentery, which brought severe diarrhoea and bleeding.

The *Hoghton Tower* ploughed her way to Iquique, arriving there in October and then fought her way home, arriving in England on a warm day in May 1892. As he disembarked in London there seemed little reason to savour the idea of another trip on the *Hoghton Tower*.

If Shackleton had missed home on his second voyage, his sisters missed him even more, and they had the house decorated with flags and banners to welcome him back. He was deeply embarrassed by the ostentation and asked the girls not to repeat the display. They promised but the promise was forgotten and subsequent returns were greeted with the same excitement.

In the weeks that followed, Shackleton was faced with a decision. He was not enamoured at the prospect of another two years apprenticeship under Robinson's iron fist. Life at home was easy and there would have been no recriminations had he opted out of his apprenticeship.

But opting out wasn't something that ever had or ever would appeal to Shackleton. Despite his qualms, he refused to admit defeat and went aboard the *Hoghton Tower* again on 27 June, bound for India.

EHS aged sixteen in 1890. He left Dulwich this year and joined the North-Western Shipping Company.

This voyage, like the previous two, began in fine, calm summer weather. It wasn't until the ship rounded the Cape of Good Hope that she was hit by storms with a ferocity that Shackleton had not previously witnessed. He did his stint at the wheel of the ship during the worst of the gales, proving himself and rising in the estimation of his superiors.

As always, his shipmates were a mixed lot with backgrounds in farming and industry, many of them running from the past. One had fled America, having committed murder. Violence was never far away and there were regular fights and the occasional stabbing on board.

In India Shackleton's task was to work on cargo, a job he thoroughly disliked. Away from the romance of the open sea, he became morose and unhappy. His lowest point came in the Bay of Mauritius where days were spent loading bagged rice by hand. This was not a part of the dream. To make matters worse, he was laid low by a virulent bout of fever. Only when the ship reached Australia did his health and temperament began to improve.

Crossing the Pacific, bound for Chile, Shackleton continued his reading and developed a habit of hanging around the ship's galley, concocting various culinary oddities involving biscuits and beef, much to the annoyance of the cook.

On the return journey they stopped at Queenstown in Cork at the end of June, and he visited relations in Moone near his birthplace in County Kildare.

Back in England, he registered for the Board of Trade examinations and studied under Captain J. Jutsum at the London Nautical School. In October 1894 he passed his examination and became a second mate.

At the end of October an old school friend, Owen Burne, took Shackleton to see the manager of the Welsh Shire Line about a job as fourth mate on the *Monmouthshire*, a tramp steamer. Shackleton was so taken aback by the condition of the fourth mate's quarters that he turned down the job. He did, however, offer to sail as a third mate and the offer was accepted, the line manager commenting that he 'rather liked him'.

On 15 November Shackleton embarked, travelling through the Mediterranean, the Indian Seas and down to China. The voyage was more placid than his storm-tossed months on the *Hoghton Tower*.

Shackleton's major responsibility was the checking of cargo. While he tended to be busy in port, the job allowed him more time to himself at sea for reading and writing.

A product of that trip is his poem 'A Tale of the Sea'. Like Mary Leadbeater, poetry was not his forte. It is, however, interesting to look at the outpourings of the twenty-two year old as he journeyed from China to Europe.

> *I slept and dreamt of the ocean:*
> *Of tarry sailors joys:*
> *Of the tales which they loved to fashion*
> *Of days when they were boys:*
> *And I laughed aloud in my sleep:*
> *"In those days they said they were men:*
> *Is there one who has a record*
> *Of worth: for a poets pen?"*
>
> *Then I saw a great long line*
> *Of ghostly ships come from the North;*
> *Come churning the seas to foam*
> *Splashing their bows with froth.*
> *Dipping now into the hollows:*

Shackleton family group c. 1894

Standing, left to right: Clara (1881-1958), attended Sydenham Girls High School, sometime clerical officer in Customs and Excise. Ernest (1874-1922). Eleanor (1879-1960), attended Sydenham Girls High School; nursed in London, New York, Winnipeg, France during World War I and Canada, where she died.

Seated in dark dresses, left to right: Ethel (1878-1935), nurse, married Rev. Frank Ayers. Amy (1875-1953), lived with family, caring for her ailing parents despite poor health, moving to Chichester to run brother Frank's antiques business. Alice (1872-1938), lived with family.

Seated in light dresses: Kathleen (1884-1961), artist, attended Sydenham Girls High School; her friend George Marston was the official artist on her brother's Nimrod and Endurance expeditions; to Canada in 1912 as artist and editor on the Montreal Star; to London during the War specializing in portraits of celebrities, and to Ireland in 1925 sketching, among others, George Russell, W.B. Yeats, G.B. Shaw, Sean O'Casey, Douglas Hyde; back to Canada c.1929 to paint Canadian Pacific Railway personnel; finally lived with sister Gladys in Dulwich, London. Gladys (1887-1962), attended Sydenham Girls High School. Helen (1882-1962), attended Sydenham Girls High School; journalist with Montreal Star and married Edmund Brietzcke in 1912.

Seated on raccoon skin rug: Francis Richard, 'Frank' (1876-1941), Royal Irish Fusiliers, Boer War 1900-01; Dublin Herald 1905 until resignation in 1907 following disappearance of 'Irish Crown Jewels'; 1913 imprisoned 15 months for fraud, later assuming a family surname Mellor; in 1930s until death ran antique shop in Chichester, in whose cemetery his inscription reads 'He lived for others', though it might be said 'He lived off others'.

> *Now on the top they rise;*
> *Pointing their booms to the oceans bed*
> *And anon to the wind swept skies.*

Like so many other things in his life, punctuation was not to be influenced by rules and regulations.

Returning in July 1895, Shackleton brought with him three baby alligators which he named Faith, Hope and Charity. These were kept in the garden pond at his parents' house until his father found a new home for them in London Zoo.

In August he was off east on the *Monmouthshire*. On this voyage he continued his paradoxical behaviour. On the one hand, he was an affable, sociable shipmate who charmed everyone on board, on the other he was studious and distant, spending long periods alone, lost in his books. He was the practical joker who, at the same time, made great efforts to persuade his companions to sign his abstinence book. He was the romantic who preferred to commune with the stars rather than visit the brothels of distant ports.

Back in London in April of 1896, he set about studying for his second-mate's examination. At the beginning of June, having passed, he immediately signed on as second mate on the *Flintshire* at a salary of £8 a month. He quickly became known on board by the nick-name 'Shacky'.

His first trip, under Captain Dwyer, was to Penang, Singapore, Hong Kong, Yokohama and San Francisco. The young dreamer had travelled a long way from the lawn of Kilkea House. This was the first of six voyages he was to make on the *Flintshire*.

On 29 June 1897 Shackleton came home for what was to prove a life-changing shore leave. He met Emily Dorman for the first time, a friend of his sister Ethel. She was twenty-nine and he was twenty-three, but the age difference didn't matter. Rather, they concentrated on the things they had in common. Both came from large families. Both shared a passion for poetry.

Emily also loved art, and as early as 1885 would write to her mother from school in Kent about her homesickness and her drawing. A letter from the same year betrays her romantic nature. Dated 14 February, it reads: 'My dearest mother … you are the only nice person in the world to me … I did so expect one Valentine at least. No one seems to know what it is to have just left home for a strict school …With love to no-one but yourself.'

EHS Master's Certificate of Competency of Foreign Trade, Singapore 28 April 1898, signed by Acting Colonial Secretary W.S. Churchill. Date and place of birth 1874, Athy, County Kildare.

Of more interest to Ernest's father, however, was the fact that her father, Charles, who practised law, had a farm in Kent where he grew orchids, something that endeared him to Shackleton senior.

Charles Dorman was a successful solicitor, a partner in the firm Kingsford Dorman which had offices close to the Law Courts on the Strand in London. He was married to Jennie Swinford who had grown up in Kent in a well-to-do but sheltered family. The couple's six children had pursued a variety of careers. The older boys, Herbert and Frank, followed their father into the law. Arthur had been ordained a Minister in the Church of England. Julia, the older of the three girls in the family, remained unmarried until she reached her forties but she was greatly taken up with the endless intrigues of her two younger sisters, Emily and Daisy, who were forever falling in and out of love.

As the nineteenth century drew to an end two things happened in the Dorman family symptomatic of middle-class life at the time. Firstly, they moved from Sydenham to the more exalted surroundings of Wetherby Gardens in South Kensington. Secondly, Charles Dorman became concerned about the state of the British empire. This concern was not unique to him, rather it was part of a wider questioning in middle England. A century of economic domination was ending and Charles Dorman suspected that the old order was changing and was anxious that his daughters should be well looked after. While he was fond of the personable Irish sailor who had befriended Emily, he was less than whelmed by the young man's prospects and by his apparent unconcern for earning a decent living.

He was also aware that Emily, while sociable and articulate, was neither as energetic nor as gregarious as the young man she was seeing. Charles Dorman was concerned about the future welfare of his daughter.

For her part, Emily appears to have seen Shackleton, initially, as a confidant rather than a prospective husband. She was coming to the end of an unhappy love affair and the seaman was prepared to listen and sympathize.

Whatever the possibilities of the relationship, they were abruptly postponed when Shackleton set sail, on 17 July, for Japan and Oregon. But now there was more on his mind than his books and his work and, when he returned to London in February 1898 for two weeks leave, he made contact with Emily and the pair visited the National Gallery and the British Museum.

Much of their time was spent discussing poets and poetry. Swinburne was then Shackleton's favourite poet and Browning was Emily's. She quickly converted him, so that, when he set off again on 11 March he took a copy of Browning's work with him.

Not that love or the prospect of love kept him from his studies. In Singapore, three days from the end of April, he was presented with his Master's Certificate in the Naval Court signed by the Colonial Secretary, Winston Churchill. By June he was home again, among his 'harem' of sisters as he called them, and close to Emily.

That shore leave was to be decisive in shaping the couple's future. While they both avoided the subject of a long-term relationship, there was almost an inevitability in its course. Emily was falling in love with Ernest but she found it difficult to say so in as many words. Even in her letters to him she constantly took one step forward and two back. Often, a letter from Emily, seeming to suggest a future for the pair, was followed immediately by another that, in trying to clarify the first, undermined whatever feeling had been expressed. Despite the obvious depth of feeling the pair had for each other, they were unable to openly declare their affection. Yet there was no question of the friendship ending.

On 27 July Ernest was off again, and the letters from Emily followed, filled with intimations of love and suggestions of doubt.

And the letters went back, from Ernest to Emily, filled with insecurity: '... I am: a man longing for the good of life which he sees shining ahead but unreachable, at least now: and the future is so uncertain that I dare hardly shape a hope.'

Back in England in the first week of December, Shackleton and Emily continued to meet. He was convinced that she was the woman for him and the Christmas season brought a new and deeper excitement than any he had experienced before. But the sailor's life was no respecter of season or sentiment and, on Christmas Day, he took ship as second mate on the *Flintshire* on a short voyage around Britain. The trip was to be even shorter than planned. The ship ran aground off Redcar on the night of 26 December. One of his shipmates, Third Engineer James Dunmore, remarked on Shackleton's interest in everything that happened that night and would later write: 'To see him once made an impression on one's mind, and my first impression was: That this man is made for something better than a captain of a small trading vessel. At that time a marked "standoffishness" existed between officers and engineers but Shackleton soon broke down the barrier which showed he was a man among men.'

As a result of the ship running aground Shackleton got leave to go home for his father's birthday. On his way he visited Emily and told her he loved her.

She wrote: 'I was deeply moved ... he put his cigarette on the ledge of the big oak chimney piece and it burnt a deep dent which we tried to rub out ... I let him out through the conservatory about 10.30 ... and he kissed my hand.'

Emily, EHS and her sister Daisy (Daedels) photographed in 1900. Daisy was an affectionate admirer of her brother-in-law Ernest to whom she referred as Mike. She died suddenly in 1916.

A week later, Shackleton was discharged from the *Flintshire*.

With the possibility of marriage now in his mind, Shackleton recognized that a career as a second mate was not going to keep Emily in any kind of comfort. He would have to look for a more rewarding career in the Merchant Navy.

A week after his discharge Shackleton wrote to the Welsh Shire Line, resigning his position. Again, through his friendship with Owen Burne, he secured a job as Fourth Officer on the *Tantallon Castle*, sailing to Cape Town.

The *Tantallon Castle* was a 3000-ton passenger liner and Shackleton found the change to his liking. The ship was comfortable and he had the opportunity to mix with the passengers and make contacts. Between March and December he made three trips on the *Tantallon* before transferring to the *Tintagel Castle*, a troop ship sailing to and from South Africa. This move was a definite improvement. His salary went up to £7 per week and he was promoted to Third Officer.

Apart from the companionship of the troops on board, Shackleton thoroughly enjoyed organizing social events and himself published a souvenir booklet, *How 1200 Soldiers went to Table Bay.*

EHS on the Tantallon Castle, 30 March 1899.

Not everything on the *Tintagel Castle* was to Shackleton's liking. When a man fell overboard, a rescue boat was launched, manned by an officer and the ship's cook. Reaching the man, the cook dived into the sea to save him. As he did, the lifeboat became unsteady and the officer also fell into the sea. All three eventually made it safely back to the ship and the officer was presented with a medal for his bravery while the cook's action was ignored. Shackleton was angered and got his sister Kathleen, the artist in the family, to do a drawing of the event which he displayed in the officer's mess as his demonstration of disapproval.

In early October 1900 Shackleton joined the Union Castle liner *Gaika* as Third Officer, with an increased salary of £8 per week. He sailed to South Africa, this time returning to England a week before Christmas to see his family and Emily.

On 5 January 1901 he boarded the *Carisbrooke Castle* and set off for the Cape, returning in mid March. This was to be his last trip as a ship's officer. On 13 March he was discharged and paid an annuity of £1/16/3, the lowest pay-off of any of the men on board.

Shackleton had many reasons for leaving the Merchant Navy. He had been working as an apprentice, a mate and an officer for eleven years and he was ready for a change. And there was the boredom factor, which constantly shadowed him. He had done what he set out to do as a teenager and, while the ocean still offered challenges, the work no longer appealed. Most important was the question of his future with Emily. Ernest wanted to marry the love of his life. Her father might see him as a likeable but poor Irish ship's officer, but he resolved nothing would stand in his way when it came to finding personal happiness.

3

Antarctica and
Polar Exploration

◆

Antarctica is not some quaint and distant piece of ice happening to house the South Pole, but the fifth largest continent on earth: 2800 miles wide and 5,500,000 square miles in area, its landmass is larger than the United States, Europe, Australia or Canada.

Unlike its northern twin, the Arctic, which is ice surrounded by a mass of land, the Antarctic is land surrounded by ice. Indeed, almost 98 per cent of the Antarctic is covered in ice. Seventy per cent of the earth's fresh water and 90 per cent of the earth's ice are locked in the frozen wastes that surround the South Pole. If all of the Antarctic's ice melted, world sea levels would rise by approximately 200 feet.

Each April, with the arrival of the southern winter, the Antarctic sea begins to freeze at a rate of up to three miles a day. By late September the continent has doubled in size, surrounded by an immense ring of sea ice, stretching from between 900 and 1000 miles in width.

The average summer temperature on the continent is 0 Celsius. In winter that temperature drops to an average of -45 Celsius. At the South Pole itself the average winter temperature is -60 Celsius. Add to this a climate that is constantly turbulent, with wind speeds of up to 180 miles an hour, and the bleakness and desolation are apparent.

There is remarkably little snowfall in the Antarctic, often as little as six inches in a year. As a result it has taken millions of years for the snowcap to reach its current state, with a depth of three miles in places and an average depth of almost a mile and a half. At 8000

Emperor Penguin from Nimrod expedition. The first written reference to penguins was by Vasco da Gama in 1499, and in 1842 James Clark Ross made the first scientific collection of Emperor penguins. Although their eggs were an important food source for early expeditions, not until the late nineteenth century were penguins exploited in large numbers for their oil, when New Zealander Joseph Hatch slaughtered hundreds of thousands of them over a twenty-five year period on the Macquarie Islands from 1891 to 1916.

feet, the average Antarctic elevation is almost three times higher than its nearest rival, Asia, and completes a landscape that is forbidding.

The very hopelessness of the continent was an essential part of its mystique. And, even if the lands offered no more than shifting, groaning ice and treacherous wind and snow storms, there was always the most basic and engaging of battles to be fought there, that between human will and the natural world.

If nothing else, Antarctica provided a place so distant from civilization that it was virtually impossible for adventurers not to be drawn into its great, white and empty heart.

For those who rose to the challenge there was further allure. The Antarctic continent wasn't entirely desolate. Life went on there, birds and fish and mammals survived. Wildlife was to be found in or close to the sea, as abundant in numbers as it was limited in diversity.

Twenty-two million penguins inhabit the Antarctic including seven of the seventeen known species, though only two – the Emperor and Adelie – are true Antarctic penguins.

The 5,000,000 Adelie penguins consume 9000 tons of shrimp per year and although they can neither fly nor sing they are ideally adapted to their environment. From the earliest landings in Antarctica, explorers have been fascinated by the behaviour of these penguins, despite their off-putting smell.

Antarctica is also home to six species of seal, among them the Fur seal, which is increasing at a rapid rate on the sub-Antarctic island of South Georgia. No longer hunted for its skin, it feeds largely on krill, which is widely available, ironically due to the virtual extinction of whales, the seals' main competitor for food in the area in the first half of the twentieth century.

Elephant Seal. Following Cook's discovery of South Georgia in 1775, huge quantities of Elephant seals and fur seals were slaughtered for oil and skins. From 1800 to1802 Edmund Fanning of New York took 57,000 fur seal skins to China.

Summer draws several types of whale to the Antarctic. Among them are the Fin-whale, weighing up to ninety tons; the Hump-back, weighing up to fifty tons; the Minke whale, weighing up to ten tons, and the Killer whale, which in fact is a type of dolphin.

The most impressive of the birds in the area is the albatross with its eleven-foot wingspan. Shackleton was to capture one of these on his 1907-09 *Nimrod* expedition and his crew blamed the bad weather, which dogged them, on its captivity.

Sperm Whale. Whaling in the Antarctic developed vigorously with the advent of explosive harpoon-heads in the 1840s. Larsen, a Norwegian, established the first whaling station in South Georgia in 1904; some 175,000 whales were killed between then and 1966.

Less impressive but more numerous are the petrels and other smaller birds which nest on the continent in summer.

The attraction of Antarctica for wildlife is due to the up-welling of nutrients along the Antarctic Convergence, where the warmer waters from the north meet the colder waters from the south. The edges of the continental islands and the waters off them provide homes in summer, in the months when the snow has melted and the ice is disintegrating.

For much of recorded history, Antarctica was simply unknown. By 150 AD, however, Ptolemy, in reaching the conclusion that the world was symmetrical, suggested the existence of a southern continent which he named *Terra Australis Incognita.* Not content with summoning this strange land from his imagination, he decreed that it was fertile and populated but cut off from the known world by a tropical zone.

In September 1578 Sir Francis Drake, aboard *The Golden Hind*, sailed through the Strait of Magellan, south of Cape Virgenes and north of Tierra del Fuego. In doing so, he proved that the Strait did not separate South America from *Terra Australis Incognita.* Rather he discovered islands to the south – among them Hoste and Los Estados. Farther south lay the ocean now known as the Drake Passage.

Thirty-eight years after Drake's voyage, in January 1616, a Dutchman, Willen Schouten, sailed around the southern tip of the islands Drake had seen. Schouten's journey from Europe had been made with a small fleet. In December 1615 one of his ships, the *Hoorn*, had been destroyed by fire while having her hull cleaned in Port Desire. Schouten decided to call the southern point of the islands after the lost ship and thus was Cape Horn named.

In 1739 a Frenchman named Bouvet thought he had located Antarctica. Given that he spent seventy days in fog and forty of those days among icebergs, with snow falling constantly, his claim is dubious.

Map of Antartica (French, c.1780). The earliest maps developed from the Egyptian geographer Ptolemy's idea of a Terra Australis Incognita. Eighteenth-century voyages by Bouvet de Lozier in the 1730s and Kerguelen in the 1770s signalled France's interest in the area. This map charts James Cook and Furneaux's voyages of the 1770s. Iles et Plaines de Glace seem predominant, and the prime meridian line passes through Paris.

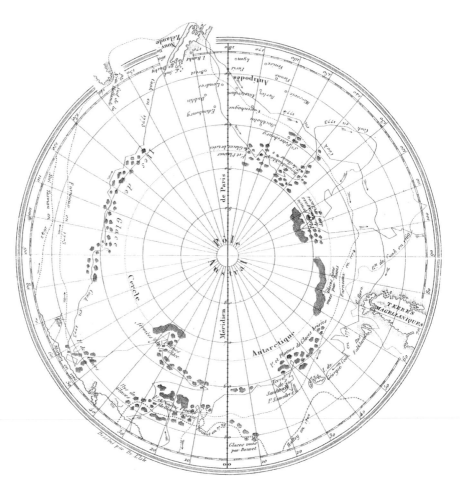

Thirty-three years later another Frenchman, Kerguelen, discovered a land he named *La France Australe*. The place was, according to Kerguelen, extremely habitable and ideal for colonization. In due course he returned with seven hundred men to colonize this new French domain. His fellow colonists, however, were less than impressed by the charms of the islands and the experiment didn't last.

48

Returning home, Kerguelen was rewarded for his misadventure with a twenty-year jail sentence.

In the same year that Kerguelen made his discovery, James Cook, a forty-four year old navigator, was setting sail from England, heading south for Antarctica.

Cook had been due to take the renowned botanist Joseph Banks with him but Banks had insisted on bringing a party of thirteen, including two French horn players. He had also insisted that Cook stop off in Madeira to pick up a third horn player, a woman.

Banks, President of the Royal Society for forty-one years, had accompanied Cook earlier on his voyage to the South Seas between 1768 and 1771. This time, however, his demands proved too much and he was left behind. His unfortunate female musician friend waited for three months in Madeira before discovering neither of them was travelling.

Captain James Cook (1728-79), a Yorkshireman, seaman and explorer, circumnavigated the world three times. First to cross the Antarctic Circle on 17 January 1773. His descriptions of large numbers of seals and whales brought the sealers south. Killed by Hawaians aged fifty.

In January 1773 Cook in HMS *Resolution* and Commander Furneaux in HMS *Adventure* took their ships across the Antarctic Circle, the first men recorded as having done so. Two years later, on 17 January 1775, Cook landed at Possession Bay in South Georgia, north of the Scotia Ridge, and claimed the island for King George III of England.

Cook was not impressed with South Georgia, describing it, with echoes of Cromwell's account of Connaught in the west of Ireland, as a 'savage and horrible country, not a tree to be seen nor a shrub even big enough to make a toothpick … doomed to perpetual frigidness' and claimed, furthermore, with all the certainty of the uninformed: 'I make bold that the world will derive no benefit from it.'

Cook never saw the southern continent but did note the large numbers of whales and seals, and his reports heralded a huge influx of British sealers and whalers into the region.

Fabian Thaddeus Bellingshausen (1787-1834), born Estonia; joined Russian Navy; probably first to sight the Antarctic continent on 27 January 1820 in ships Vostok *and* Mirnyi. *(Central Navy Museum, Leningrad)*

The first British sealers to arrive in South Georgia came in 1786 and so began a trade that was to peak in the nineteenth century with over 1100 recorded sealing expeditions. Many other voyages were not recorded to keep them secret from competitors.

In the two-year period from 1800, Edmund Fanning, a New York sealer, took 57,000 fur seal-skins from South Georgia alone, bringing them directly to China, where they were sold at a huge profit for felt-making. Indeed in the early years of the nineteenth century millions of seals were slaughtered in the Antarctic.

On 27 January 1820 the Russian Fabian Thaddeus Bellingshausen unwittingly made the first sighting of Antarctica. Bellingshausen, an admirer of Cook, circumnavigated Antarctica and crossed the Antarctic Circle six times in his ships the *Vostok* and the *Mirnyi*.

Coincidentally, three days after Bellingshausen's sighting, Edward Bransfield, a Cork-born sailor who had been pressganged into the British Navy, also sighted the continent and charted the north-west end of the peninsula, naming it the Trinity Land.

Apart from his discovery work, Bellingshausen had advanced views on health and hygiene. All his crew-members had to be under thirty-five years of age and extremely fit. One of the ways in which he maintained the men's health and fitness was by organizing regular saunas for them, with steam-rooms heated by hot cannon balls.

On one trip he collected thirty penguins, some of which were eaten and the rest kept in chicken runs and bathtubs, being fed on pork before they died. The skins of the dead penguins were used to make caps and their fat was used for greasing boots.

Bellingshausen also met Nathaniel Palmer, a Connecticut-born sealer, in 1820 and, on 16 November of that year Palmer, and the crew of his ship, *Hero*, also sighted the Davis Coast of the Antarctic Peninsula. Bellingshausen's achievements were to go unpublicized, and a century was to pass before he received due recognition.

Insofar as it's possible to date the first landing on the Antarctic continent, and despite later well-publicized claims, the honour appears to go Captain John Davis, a sealer from the United States of America, who landed at Hughes Bay on the Antarctic Peninsula on 7 February 1821.

In 1823 James Weddell took his two ships, *Jane* and *Beaufoy*, on an expedition that married his sealing interest with exploration. Weddell was an inspired leader of men and committed to the latest and best in available scientific instrumentation. With the benefit of warm weather, Weddell pushed over two hundred miles farther south than Cook had done. Such was the regard in which Weddell was held that the sea into which he took his ships was later named for him.

Eight years later two British sailors, Biscoe and Avery, circumnavigated Antarctica. The pair worked for the Enderby Brothers as sealers but, like Weddell, they shared a keen interest in exploration and their work confirmed the status of Antarctica as a continent.

In 1838 the French made another investigative foray south. This voyage was led by Admiral Jules Dumont d'Urville, a native of Calvados. D'Urville was a gifted explorer who discovered the Venus de Milo on the island of Milos. In 1840 he planted the French flag on an island off the Antarctic coast, being unable to land on the mainland. He named the land for his wife, Terre Adelie. She had accompanied him and they celebrated the naming with

a bottle of Bordeaux before almost losing their lives in a horrific storm. D'Urville also named the Adelie penguin for his wife.

As he made his way home he met the New York adventurer Charles Wilkes, in his ship *The Porpoise* heading south. Wilkes had a much tougher trip than d'Urville and he lost 119 of his crew of 342. Wilkes claimed the existence of land in areas James Clark Ross was later to sail over. On his return, he was welcomed with a court-martial. Apart from the magnitude of his imagination, Wilkes left one abiding contribution to the history of the exploration of the southern continent, naming it the Antarctic.

James Weddell (1787-1834), Scottish explorer and sealer, voyaged to Antarctica on the Jane *and* Beaufoy *1819-24. Sailed into the Weddell Sea, naming the South Orkney Islands; the Weddell seal was also named for him.*

The next important expedition was led the following year, 1839, by Sir James Ross, a Scot who had joined the Royal Navy as a boy of twelve years. In 1831, sailing with his uncle, Sir John Ross, they had located the Magnetic North Pole.

Ross was charged with making measurements of the earth's magnetic field and his was the first expedition into waters that were to become known as the Ross Sea.

Ross set a new farthest South record of 78 degrees, a record that remained unbeaten until 1900.

Ross and his crew caught Emperor penguins and wrote the first biological account of the contents of the birds' stomachs. He went on to describe and name 500 miles of new coastline, discovering the Transantarctic Mountains, the Ross Ice Shelf, Ross Island and two volcanoes, which he named Erebus and Terror, after his ships.

The commander of the *Terror* was Francis Crozier, who was born in 1796 in Banbridge, Co. Down. Crozier died on board ship in 1848 when, as commander, he took part in Sir John Benjamin Franklin's expedition to discover the North-West Passage.

Erebus, *built 1826, captained by James Clark Ross, and* Terror, *built 1813, captained by Francis Crozier 1839-43. Engraving depicts near-disaster off Antactica on 13 March 1842.*

In 1874 the modern age of steam made its impact on the southern continent. *The Challenger*, a steam-ship and floating laboratory, crossed the Antarctic Circle that year. The earliest known photographs of ice-bergs were taken from its deck. Later the ship was involved in oceanographic work in the North Pacific, taking ocean soundings to a depth of 26,850 feet.

Francis Rawdon Moira Crozier (1796-1848), born Banbridge, Co. Down, Ireland. After his trip with Ross he went with Sir John Franklin's ill-fated expedition to find the North-West Passage. Both ships, Erebus and Terror, were lost and all 129 men died.

Left: Crozier Memorial, Bambridge, built in 1862 at a cost of £700.

Between 1893 and 1895 a Nor-wegian sealing and whaling expedition, led by Henrik Bull, who lived in Australia, reached the Ross Sea in its search for whales. On 24 January 1895 Captain Kristensen and Carsten Borchgrevink each claimed to be the first to land on the continent. Borchgrevink enhanced his claim by drawing a picture of the landing. The ship, *The Antarctic*, was subsequently crushed and sank off Paulet Island on the Nordenskjold expedition of 1903.

This regular but unco-ordinated succession of discoveries in the Antarctic meant little to most people. Even within geographic circles, the Antarctic was far from top of the agenda. All of that was to change, however.

The Sixth International Geographical Congress of 1895, held in London, revived interest in the exploration of Antarctica and signalled the beginning of what was to become known as the Heroic Age of Antarctic Exploration.

Between 1897 and 1899 a Belgian expedition, led by Adrien de Gerlache – who was later to act as an interpreter of Shackleton's lecture to the Royal Society of Brussels and also provided the *Endurance* for him in 1914 – explored the Antarctic Peninsula and when his ship became stuck in ice, he and his crew were forced to overwinter on the ice, south of the Antarctic Circle, the first men to do this. So desperate were conditions that the crewmen were forced to pile snow up and around the deck of the ship, forming a virtual igloo in order to maintain what little warmth there was.

Interestingly, among the international party on board the *Belgica* were Roald Amundsen

and Dr Frederick Cook. Amundsen discovered the North-West Passage in 1905 and led the first group to reach the South Pole in December 1911, while Cook was to claim to be the first man to reach the North Pole in 1908. Whatever about the veracity of Amundsen's claim, there were serious doubts cast over Cook's.

De Gerlache and his men achieved the recognition of scientists and geographers as the first group to spend the winter on their ice-bound ship. The achievement, however, also brought serious pressures. The isolation and the uncertainty got to some of De Gerlache's crew. One man climbed off the ship onto the ice and told his startled shipmates that he was off to Belgium.

Despite these personal traumas, the crew of the *Belgica* carried out numerous experiments from their winter quarters and took the earliest known photographs of the continent.

Carsten Borchgrevink returned to Antartica in 1898, this time aboard the *Southern Cross* and leading his own expedition. Borchgrevink's trip was largely sponsored by the British publisher Sir George Newnes, who made much of his money through his populist publications, including the sensationalist *Tit Bits* magazine. Not surprisingly Sir Clements Markham, President of the Royal Geographical Society, was unimpressed by Newnes donating money to an expedition led by a Norwegian, and it spurred him on in the planning of his own British Antarctic expedition.

Borchgrevink – an opportunist and an egoist – was especially unpopular on the *Southern Cross*. There were regular disagreements between him and his fellow expedition members.

At one point he dismissed William Colbeck, an extremely well-qualified navigator, and then asked him to stay on as a guest. Another crew member, Klovstad, was dismissed and reinstated a few days later. Bernacchi, who later travelled on the *Discovery* expedition, wrote of Borchgrevink that he grinned 'in an imbecilic manner ... [and] made use of some coarse, ill-bred remarks – language of the gutter'.

The biologist Hanson died in the course of the *Southern Cross* expedition. Hanson had become fascinated and enthralled by the behaviour of the penguins in Antarctica and had waited for their return to breed, before dying – with a penguin on his chest. Such were the conditions that his colleagues were forced to use dynamite to dig his grave.

Later, on his *Nimrod* expedition, Shackleton was to include nine dogs descended from the dogs used by Borchgrevink.

Much of the work done by the expeditions to the Antarctic was cartographic. As the expeditions pushed south, mapping was a regular part of the work undertaken, though it wasn't until the advent of Antarctic flight that the mapping could finally be completed.

The first man to fly by aeroplane above the Antarctic was Hubert Wilkins, a member of Shackleton's last *Quest* expedition. He did this in November 1928 and a month later flew over the Antarctic Peninsula, a journey of 1300 miles, which took eleven hours to complete. During the flight, Wilkins took a large number of photographs of the continent below him.

Eventually, in 1946, the United States organized Operation Highjump, using 4700 men and 13 ships, as well as aircraft, to take 3260 metres of cine-film of three-quarters of the perimeter of the continent. They also took 65,000 aerial photographs of Antarctica and finally put to rest the fanciful theory of the nineteenth-century American eccentric, John Symmes, that the earth was hollow and open at the poles.

4

South with Scott

1901–1903

The dawn of the twentieth century was to prove momentous for Ernest Shackleton. He had reached a point in his life where decisions needed to be made. He was determined to marry Emily Dorman and felt she was of like mind, but he was also eager not to spend the rest of his working life in the Merchant Navy.

In the early summer of 1900, while Shackleton was on leave from his ship, he saw an article in the London *Times* about an Antarctic expedition being planned by Robert F. Scott. Shackleton's membership of the Royal Geographical Society allowed him to know that, while Scott might lead the expedition, the man behind the plan was Sir Clements Markham, President of the Royal Geographical Society.

Markham was adamant, in spite of government and Royal Navy disinterest, that Britain should remain to the fore in exploration. The idea that foreigners might lead the race to the South Pole incensed him and he saw the Royal Navy as the answer to Britain's problem.

Markham was well used to finding little sympathy in the upper echelons of the Royal Navy but, in 1898, the Royal Geographical Society had organized a meeting about Antarctica. Sir John Murray had suggested a number of areas, including meteorology, glacial studies, geology and coastal surveys, in which an expedition might prove worthwhile. The following year Markham announced plans for an expedition to Antarctica. A successful trip would, he was convinced, restore confidence in the Royal Navy and in Britain's reputation.

Not that Markham was alone in his view that Britain deserved better. Queen Victoria's reign was drawing to a close and her years on the throne had seen the British empire spread and consolidate. Yet there was a feeling, which Markham shared, that Britain was in danger of being left behind by other, more eager nations. The boundless optimism of the late nineteenth century was slowly being eroded by the Boer War. It was clear that Victoria could not reign forever and minds were already turning to life under Edward. Empire or not, Britain's glory was looking in need of a new burst of energy, enthusiasm and, above all, achievement. Markham's patriotic concerns were, however, constrained by snobbery. His initial insistence that the expedition be manned from the Royal Navy was based on a contempt for the Merchant Navy. However, without the support of the government

Sir Clements Markham (1830-1916), another Yorkshireman; President of the Royal Geographical Society 1893-1905; determined and obstinate instigator of Scott's Discovery *expedition; in later years went strongly against Shackleton. Related to the Irish Clements family.*

and with only £5000 available through the RGS, he was forced to turn to private sponsorship and this was where Ernest Shackleton found his opening.

He already felt that life was passing him by. His brother Frank had enlisted in the Royal Irish Fusiliers and gone to South Africa. Exploration seemed to offer a means of finding the finances to impress Emily's father. A lecture in London by Borchgrevink in the summer of 1900 reinforced that sentiment. Finance and adventure, it appeared, lay to the south.

Among the passengers Shackleton befriended in his time sailing to South Africa was Cedric Longstaff, whose father Llewllyn emerged as one of the major sponsors of the planned Antarctic expedition. Through Cedric, Shackleton met Longstaff senior and impressed him with his friendliness and his energy. Longstaff got in touch with Markham and let it be known that he was anxious for Shackleton to join the expedition. Markham could hardly refuse – £25,000, a quarter of the estimated budget for a three-year expedition, depended on Longstaff's generosity.

Markham asked Albert Armitage, who was to be Scott's second-in-command, to make enquiries about Shackleton and this he did, to his own and Markham's satisfaction. In February he was appointed as a member of the expedition while away at sea on the *Carisbrook Castle*. In March he learned of his appointment and of his leave from the shipping line. Markham salved his own patriotic conscience by getting Shackleton a commission in the Royal Navy Reserve.

In the meantime Markham and Scott were forging ahead with plans. Scott had been chosen for his youth – he was thirty-two at the time – his commitment and, presumably, his inexperience, which allowed Markham to command the details of the expedition as he wished. He suggested the route *Discovery* might take and where she might berth for the winter. Scott would be Markham's proxy in Antarctica.

In Scott, Shackleton was meeting a man who was, in some ways, a reflection of himself, but also a man who was radically different. Each was ambitious and young, but where Scott was introvert, Shackleton was outgoing. And where Scott was a product of the Royal Navy and a protégé of the ostentatious and overbearing Markham, Shackleton was very much a Merchant Navy man and possessed of a strong Irish strain of independence and egalitarianism. One was a businessman, the other something of an idealist.

Scott was the son of an easy-going father and a deeply religious mother. As a child he had been a dreamer with twin aversions to the sight of blood and cruelty to animals. He made his first voyage in 1883, at the age of thirteen. His experience of life at sea had, like Shackleton's, shown him that while a young boy's dreams might be of adventure, the reality was a life of hard work and danger. In 1891 he began training on HMS *Vernon*, a torpedo ship. Three years later his father went bankrupt and was forced to find a job as a brewery manager. By 1897 he was dead, leaving his two sons to support the rest of the family.

Poverty set Scott aside from his friends and was responsible for a secretive nature that was to be an integral part of his character.

In 1898 Scott lost his brother Archie to typhoid fever. The responsibility for keeping the family solvent now lay on his shoulders alone.

A year later he met Markham, learned of the forthcoming Antarctic expedition and applied for a place on it. He had, according to himself, 'no urge towards snow or ice' but he did want 'freedom to develop more widely'. Markham put forward the names of three men as possible leaders, Commander John de Robeck, Charles Royds and Scott. Scott and Royds were released by the Navy and, following what some members of the selection

The Discovery, *over wintering in McMurdo Sound. The classic Antarctic ship, purpose-built in Dundee, Scotland, at a cost of £34,050, for Scott's 1901-04* Discovery *expedition. Later used in the Arctic and for scientific research work. Now open to the public in Dundee.*

committee saw as Markham's high-handedness, Scott was appointed leader. Markham believed he had found the man to direct the expedition, a man who possessed 'the very same qualities that are needed in the stress of battle'. Only later was his suitability as a leader called into question.

Whatever unease Shackleton may have felt at encountering the expedition leader soon disappeared. He wanted to make the best of the opportunity Longstaff had procured for him, and he quickly settled into the offices of the expedition in Burlington Gardens in London.

Being on land also meant he could see Emily regularly. Now that he had a career, he felt that his chances of impressing her and her father were greatly enhanced.

Markham was struck by Shackleton's manner and ability and welcomed him as a regular guest at his home in Eccleston Square. Shackleton, on his part, avoided the infighting that went on between the Royal Geographical Society, the Navy, the Royal Society and the government, which had now come in with a grant of £45,000.

The vessel built to carry the expeditionary group was the *Discovery*, a 172-foot, 1620-ton, steel-plated, coal- and sail-powered ship. She had been launched in Dundee on 21 March and now, as the summer arrived, Shackleton was sent to her trials off the Scottish coast in the Firth of Tay.

Back in London, Shackleton realized that while the plans for the expedition might be advanced, much practical work had been left undone. Markham was impressed by his attention to detail. Nothing was too banal. He organized a collection of wigs and dresses – for the theatricals that were to be part of the long winter nights in Antarctica – and ensured there was a typewriter for the typing of an on-board newspaper.

In June *Discovery* arrived in London and the level of excitement in the expedition offices began to rise. Shackleton was appointed third mate and given responsibility for stowing the ship. When the final list of officers and crew of the *Discovery* was drawn up, Shackleton's biography appeared as follows, including a mistaken birth date:

'5. Third Lieutenant – ERNEST SHACKLETON, born 4 November 1874. He entered the Merchant Service in 1890, and served in sailing ships in the Pacific, afterwards in the *Castle* line. *Sub-Lieut.*, R.N.R. F.R.G.S. In charge of sea-water analysis. Ward room caterer. In charge of the holds, stores, and provisions, and arranges and serves out provisions. He also arranges the entertainments.'

As departure day drew nearer, Shackleton was sent for a short training-course in balloon-ing at Aldershot and on a detonation course on the Thames estuary. The detonation was for the practical purpose of learning how to free the ship from ice and the ballooning was to prepare him for aerial photography.

Shackleton was initiated as a Freemason on 9 July 1901 in the Navy Lodge No. 2612, London. On 30 May 1913 he was raised in the Guild of Freemen, Lodge No. 3535. He was a member of both lodges until his death. He probably viewed this as another step up in society and might well have argued that it was a harmless one, but it sits uneasily with the image of the laughing, carefree Irishman he promoted. The Freemasons were a secret society who portrayed themselves – when they admitted to membership at all – as a charitable and positive organization. Their exclusivity was at odds with the idea of a man like Shackleton, supposedly at one with the world.

About this time, Emily informed Shackleton that she was in love with another, unnamed young man. Rather than run from this news, he appears to have decided to spread his dreams before her and risk rejection in vying for her affection.

'I said it in the old days "Love me a little only a little",' he wrote. '... as I grow older I am saying "Love me altogether and only me" ... I have nothing to offer you: I am poor: I am not clever, it is wicked of me to want you to keep caring for me ... Why did you not tremble to my touch first of all the men in this world.'

Whether Shackleton moved Emily with his words, or whether she had already grown tired of the other love in her life, by the time *Discovery* sailed in July 1901 he was convinced that she would marry him.

He had asked that the family not come to see him off. Instead, three of his sisters – Helen, Kathleen and Gladys – were at the Albert Docks and he signalled his farewell to them using semaphore flags.

The crew of *Discovery* were leaving behind a country supportive of their endeavours, but not overly so. The British newspapers wrote positively of the expedition, the govern-ment had come up with some money, and most people wished the expedition well, but there was little of the flag-waving that might have been expected.

Shackleton – once safely on board – wrote to Emily's father, asking for her hand in marriage. The letter is a mixture of hope and ambition.

My dear Mr Dorman,

I must thank you very much for all your good wishes for the coming voyage. I would like to tell you in this letter that it is mainly for one reason that I am going is to get on so that when I come back or later when I have made money I might with your permission marry Emily if she still cares for me then as I feel she does now; it is needless to say that I care for her more than anyone else in the world but I fully see the difficulties in the way as regards my not having money but time will overcome that and you will not object if I have sufficient and keep her as you would wish. I can see well how you must look at my wanting always to be with Emmie knowing that my circumstances are not rosey and I can only thank you for your goodness in allowing me to see so much of her. If she cares for me later and you can see that I may honestly marry her I would be ever happy. I have of course spoken to her all these years but only lately has she I think really cared altogether for me. However she will talk to you ... for me my future is all to make but I intend making it quickly. I would have spoken to you myself before only Emily had not given me a full answer. Now I feel it is all right so am asking you not now but when I make money or position and money to marry her.

Yours sincerely,
Ernest H Shackleton.

It says much of his character that he was prepared to wait for word until such time as a reply caught up with him. It also suggests that he was less than optimistic and that a rejection on the page might be more bearable than one coming face to face.

After King Edward VII had come aboard and wished the crew well, *Discovery* set off. Shackleton quickly made friends with Hugh Robert Mill, brought along at the last minute to put some order on the ship's library between England and Madeira, where he would leave and return home. Mill also taught him how to determine the density and salinity of seawater. Years later he would note that Shackleton found this work 'rather irksome, and was long in grasping the importance of writing down one reading of an instrument before making the next'.

As the voyage progressed, it became apparent that *Discovery* was slow and not totally suited to the trip in hand. She leaked in several places, creating problems for Shackleton as he was responsible for the stowing of supplies. But there were greater problems with Scott who seemed unable to relate to his men and alienated many of the crew, particularly those used to the more relaxed ways of the Merchant Navy.

After *Discovery* left Madeira, Shackleton became a close friend of Edward Wilson, the junior surgeon. Wilson was a good listener and Shackleton a good talker, and the pair enjoyed each other's company. Shackleton thought Wilson needed looking after and bought him matting to lie on in the tropical heat.

'He has quite taken me in charge,' Wilson noted. For his part, Wilson curbed Shackleton's wilder excesses and kept him out of trouble. Often, the pair sat on deck, in the afternoon sun, reading poetry and talking. When it came to work, Shackleton regularly helped Wilson with his notation of birds.

While he kept himself busy with work, Emily was constantly in Shackleton's thoughts and her father's reaction to his request for her hand hung uncertainly over him. Eventually, the long-awaited letter arrived.

My dear Ernest,

I have received your letter of the 3rd. I quite appreciate all you say and was not the least surprised to read it. I sincerely and heartily wish you a safe voyage and a happy return some 2 or 3 years hence having accomplished the arduous task before you and that you will be able to tell us what the Antarctic really is. I can only say now that if & whenever the time comes when you are in the pecuniary position you long for & that if you & Emmy are still of the same mind my consent to your union will not be wanting – with all good wishes.

I am yours sincerely,
Chas Dorman.

Ironically, by the time the *Discovery* docked in New Zealand and Shackleton received the letter, Charles Dorman was dead.

New Zealand offered a chance for the scientific staff on the expedition to get away from the ship but, for Shackleton and his fellow sailors there was work to be done on board, stowing supplies and settling the pack of dogs Scott had agreed to take. Shackleton was also given responsibility for forty-five sheep donated by New Zealand farmers.

On 24 December 1901 the *Discovery* left Lyttelton on the final and most important leg of its journey south. Three days later, on Christmas Eve, New Zealand faded from sight.

The early days of the New Year saw *Discovery* sailing calmly through quiet waters, the weather settled, and then the crew saw their first icebergs. Louis Bernacchi, one of the scientists on the ship, described the men's reaction to their first sight of Antarctica: 'It was a scene of fantastic and unimagined beauty and we remained on deck till morning.'

For Shackleton and others who had never before had this experience, there was an intense feeling of exhilaration. This was a new seascape. First came the strange glow in the sky, the reflected light bouncing off ice and snow. Then the sight of the ice floes themselves, huge mountains of white that radiated greens and blues as they glided by. And, finally, the sound of the grinding of ice as berg pushed against berg. And then another sound, like waves on shingle, of water breaking on pack ice. Everything was new, everything was fresh and sharp and promising. There was a sense that a step had been taken and nothing could ever be the same about life again, as the men stayed on deck to see and hear and wonder at the new continent.

Discovery made good time, even through the pack ice facing her at the Ross Sea. Apart from the dogs taken to draw sledges, the expedition had also been equipped with skis, though no one knew how to use them properly. Scott devised a system of learning as they went. Men would leave the ship and step onto the ice floes to practice skiing, something Shackleton never mastered.

On 9 January Shackleton was among the first party to land at Cape Adare. An ambition had been achieved. The party left a note for any relief ship that might follow, deposited, as arranged, in a hut built by Borchgrevink's party two years earlier.

From this point, *Discovery* sailed along the coast, through the muttering icebergs, reaching

Wood Bay – Markham's suggested landing-point, only to find it frozen over. Two days later Shackleton led a geological party onto the ice and, to their great excitement, discovered moss, the farthest south any moss had then been found.

At the end of the month *Discovery* came within sight of Mount Erebus and continued east along the Great Ice Barrier. By the second last day of January they were in territory unseen by previous explorers. They discovered and named King Edward VII Land for the new king.

It was, as Shackleton noted, a 'unique sort of feeling'. Hopes were high.

On 31 January *Discovery* sailed into a snare of icebergs. By evening the ship was completely trapped. It was to be almost twelve hours before she broke free.

Scott's handling of the crisis impressed few of the men. It seemed to many that he had panicked in the face of danger.

Immediately after their escape, Scott called the crew together and informed them they would winter in the Antarctic. Shackleton was overjoyed. He had feared that *Discovery* might be turned north and the expedition curtailed.

Before finding a winter home, Scott took *Discovery* into an inlet in the Barrier and arranged for ballooning trips. Scott, despite the fact that he had no training, was first to ascend in the balloon, nicknamed *Eva*, followed by Shackleton who, to his delight went higher than the Captain, reaching an altitude of 800 feet and taking the first aerial photographs on the continent, achievements that were medal ribbons to his mind.

Moving on, Scott brought the ship close to Mount Erebus on Ross Island and decided this was where they would winter. The plan was for the ship to be frozen in, making her stable until spring. This took longer than anticipated. Storms constantly broke the surrounding ice and it was some time before *Discovery* was finally part of the continent to which she had delivered her crew.

Shackleton remained busy, overseeing stores, continuing his water-testing duties, arranging for the slaughter of the sheep which were then hung up to be frozen. The state of the stores concerned him: 'I am rather worried about some of our food for instead of being in good condition for the winter the vegetables got from Germany have turned out to be in a wretched state … We will have the mutton … every Sunday. And seal for all hands every second day. So there ought to be no chance of scurvy.'

The men settled quickly into the routine of being at sea but being on land. *Discovery* became their home but they could spend much of their time on the frozen continent. Scientific experiments continued and the men continued their skiing practice – in Shackleton's case without any noticeable improvement. He was also charged with training the dogs, at which he was equally unsuccessful.

In mid-February he was chosen, with Wilson and the Dublin-born geologist Ferrar, to make the first exploratory steps towards the Pole, in a trial expedition to White Island.

Unable to control the dogs or to ski properly, the three men set off walking, flags flying from their sledge. While the dogs stayed behind the three men trudged through the snow, expending energy on pulling a sledge which might have been pulled by the animals, walking when they might have skied much more easily.

Having a flag with the family motto, *Fortitudine Vincimus*, was more important, at least in Markham's mind when he planned the expedition, than having dogs which obeyed their masters, or sleeping-bags that kept out the cold. Shackleton might set off in the spirit which Markham had fostered, but he would quickly learn that practicality was more important to survival than the symbolic needs of a distant overseer.

Shackleton and his comrades learned that distances can be deceiving in a polar desert. Heading south-east and into the face of snowstorms, they soon suffered from frostbite. Twelve-hour marches with little or no food, time spent in a tent with no sleeping-bags and insufficient rations, were salutary lessons in the realities of exploration.

And there were other lessons. Socks soaked in sweat froze to boots. Tiredness meant that risks were taken. The three climbed, without being roped, to the top of the mountain they had set out to climb. There were falls into crevasses that might, but for luck, have ended in death or serious injury. Had not the dangers been so real, the whole thing might have been farcical.

The return journey took just eleven hours and Shackleton, when he reached *Discovery*, could not be kept from telling and re-telling every detail of the march. It wasn't long before his shipmates grew tired of his tales.

If that expedition had been blessed, another, which set out on 4 March, did not end so fortunately. A group led by Lieutenant Michael Barne became lost in fog and one of its members, a sailor named George Vince, slid to his death over a cliff.

Left: Sledging flags for the Discovery expedition. Despite the design being clearly specified by Markham, the square Shackleton flag stood out defiant and conspicuous in its difference.

Opposite: Balloon trip; on 4 February 1902, on the ice edge at the Bay of Whales, nineteen cylinders of gas were used to inflate the balloon Eva. Scott went up first followed by Shackleton to a height of 800 feet to take the first Antarctic aerial photographs. Ted Wilson thoroughly disapproved, writing in his diary: ' ... if some of these experts don't come to grief over it out here it will only be because God has pity on the foolish.'

THE

S ᴏᴜᴛʜ Pᴏʟᴀʀ Tɪᴍᴇs.

ᴀᴘʀɪʟ · 1902

Title page of first issue of *South Polar Times*, April 1902

'The South Polar Times' title-page.

Deep winter was now drawing in as the men settled into their quarters. A hut was erected on the ice giving the place its name, Hut Point. The intention had been that, should the ship move back north for the winter, some men might live in this but, with the crew settled on board ship, the hut was used as a store.

Shackleton spent many of the dark days editing five issues of the ship's paper, *The South Polar Times*. The first issue was 'published' on 23 April 1902. For others, only work and occasional recreation, mainly draughts and shove-ha'penny, broke the long dreary winter. The scientists among the crew continued their studies, but the pressure of living together led to regular squabbles. Wilson, who had recovered from tuberculosis, insisted on taking a daily walk and Shackleton, generally, accompanied him, thus escaping much on-ship bickering.

Royal Navy men and Merchant Navy men were not particularly comfortable with each other and Scott's strong disciplinarian streak continued to irk his more easy-going colleagues. Shackleton, on the other hand, could be found in conversation in all quarters, with all of the crew.

In spite of the conflict and class division, four months of darkness passed without major incident. Shackleton's main concern was whether he would be chosen for the party heading south when the weather improved. He recognized that some of his colleagues might see this as arrogance, but he resolved to be in the group.

Initially, Scott had decided that two men would make the journey, but Wilson had persuaded him, sensibly, that a third was necessary. Should one become ill or be injured, a third person would give the party a greater chance of getting back safely. Finally, on 13 June, Scott informed the crew that the southern party would consist of three men – Wilson, Shackleton and himself.

It is not surprising that the final preparations for the push south were as ineffectual as most of what had gone before. Whether Scott believed luck and providence would take the party safely to the Pole and back is unclear. Wilson seems to have been the only one fully alive to the dangers that lay ahead.

Scientific experiments continued around *Discovery* in the days before their departure, yet the more important preparations were never made. None of the three men had mastered the dogs, so Shackleton was delegated to work with them but had neither the patience nor understanding to win their respect. Indeed, he spent much of his time perfecting a go-cart, a sledge on wheels driven by a sail, which proved impractical in the soft snow.

A trial run with the dogs earlier in September proved useless. The animals refused to pull the sledges and, to all intents and purposes, went their own way. Even then, no one faced the fact that the dog training was a necessity.

On another run, men, sledges and dogs constantly fell into crevasses. Again, the chaos was ignored and Scott returned to the ship ahead of the training party. The men were unimpressed by the notion of a captain abandoning men in trouble.

Scott, meanwhile, had other problems to deal with. Albert Armitage, his second-in-command, was bitterly disappointed at not being included in the expeditionary party. He'd accompanied Scott on the understanding that he would be one of the south party and now felt betrayed. The atmosphere between the captain and his deputy was tense.

To add to their troubles, Shackleton, among others, appeared to be suffering from a mild dose of scurvy. Scurvy had long been the curse of sailors. We now know it owes its origins to a lack of Vitamin C but, at the beginning of the twentieth century vitamins were unknown and the treatment for the disease altogether more uncertain. What were clear were the symptoms – swollen gums, the passing of blood and general debility. The absence of fresh vegetables and a diet limited to salted meat were among the main causes of scurvy and, while most sailors overcame the disease, they knew it could be a killer. Like so many other issues, this problem was not faced and it was presumed that everything would turn out all right.

Scott was so secretive about the expedition south that Wilson and Shackleton were informed of the date of leaving a week before departure. This led to a rush to finalize arrangements. Stores and sledges were prepared, and a last effort was made to get the dogs under

On 2 November 1902, left to right, Shackleton, Scott and Wilson before they set out on their southern journey.

control, but Shackleton abandoned this to complete the latest issue of the *South Polar Times* and to try to learn to use a theodolite, a skill Scott had forgotten to tell him he needed. Clothing was sorted and letters written to loved ones in the knowledge that the journey about to be undertaken could be the last the three men would make. With their lack of experience and the fact that they were facing the unknown, the shadow of possible death hung over them. Only their ignorance and bravado threw light on their situation.

The day before he left, Shackleton wrote a letter to Emily, intended to be read only in the event of his death.

Beloved I hope you may never have to read this, but darling loved one it comes to you. You will know that your lover left this world with all his hearts yours his last thoughts will be of you my own dear Heart, Child I am carrying your little photo with me South and so your face will be with me to the last: Child remember that I am your true lover, that you and you alone have been in my heart and mind all this time. Beloved do not grieve for me for it has been a man's work and I have helped my little mite towards the increase of knowledge: Child there are millions in this world who have not had this chance. You will always remember me my own true woman and little girl. I cannot say more my heart is so full of love and longing for you and words will not avail, they are so poor in such a case. Child we may meet again in another world, and I believe in God, that is all I can say, but it covers all things: I have tried to do my best as a man the rest I leave to Him. And if there is another world and he wills it we shall find each other. I feel that there must be. This cannot be the end, but I do not know, I only believe from something in me. Yet again I cannot tell if there is, I hope. Child you will comfort those at home. Know once more that I love you truly and purely and as dearly as a woman can be loved. And now my true love goodnight. Your lover, ERNEST.

Child take the little things I send you and take what you want from home.
God bless you and keep you safe forever.

The following morning, Sunday 2 November, Scott, Wilson and Shackleton posed for photographs before setting off. The triangular pennants designed by Markham fluttered from the sledges – except in Shackleton's case. He had designed his own rectangular flag, which showed up much better in photographs.

The plan – according to Scott – was to make a thirteen-week journey. For the first week a back-up party would accompany them. After that the three would go on alone.

Initially there were fewer problems than might have been expected. Amazingly, the dogs who had refused to work earlier were now reasonably well behaved. Progress in the first week went well, men and animals were acclimatizing themselves to the snow. The only real problem seemed to be a cough which Shackleton had suddenly developed.

The departure of the back-up party coincided with a blizzard, leaving the men temporarily snowed in. When the weather cleared and the three pushed on, the dogs became impossible to handle, hardly surprising on starvation rations. To make matters worse, they were harnessed together and pulling all the sledges, in a train, a weight of one and a half tons. Only by pulling with them – a cardinal error in controlling a dog team – could the three

Ted and Oriana Wilson. The Wilson family were friends of Dr William Shackleton in Bushey, Hertfordshire. When Dr Shackleton met Captain Scott on a visit to the Terra Nova, Wilson smoothed this awkward encounter. (Peggy Larken, who met Shackleton aged five in 1913)

make any progress. Very quickly, given the weight of the sledges, it became necessary to relay the loads. This meant taking some of the sledges to a point and then returning for the remainder, so that every mile forward involved three miles of walking. The men's progress dropped at times to as little as two and a half miles a day.

To add to difficulties none of the three had properly mastered skiing and their skis sat, virtually useless, on the sledges. They made efforts to learn as they went but, like so much about the expedition, it was all too little and too late.

Nor were these practicalities the most serious of their troubles. Wilson noticed that Scott and Shackleton shared a deep distrust of each other. Shackleton was unimpressed by his leader, Scott was threatened by his companion. The irritation finally sparked one night while Shackleton was preparing a meal in their tent. He accidentally overturned the stove, spilling the food and burning a hole in the groundsheet. Scott was apoplectic and the emotions which both had kept under control were immediately out in the open, angry voices echoing across the frozen emptiness. Wilson eventually placated the pair and an uneasy truce was called.

When Shackleton and Scott weren't squabbling or pulling the sledges across the wilderness or sleeping, they read aloud, in turns, in their tent. Their moods ebbed and flowed and only Wilson's patience kept the peace. At one point Scott, faced with physical and emotional fatigue, suggested turning back. Wilson dissuaded him.

As they moved on, Wilson developed other concerns about his companions. He was worried about their health. Shackleton had been coughing continuously through the first month of the expedition, keeping the others awake at night. By December he seemed to be losing energy and showed signs of scurvy. Scott, while not as ill, was also showing signs of the disease. Still living on minimum rations, men and dogs were already severely malnourished. In a month they had covered just over a hundred miles. It was a time for hard decisions.

Scott concluded that they must leave as much of the food as possible at a depot, marked with a flag so that they could collect the supplies on the return.

Given that the dogs were still proving of little use in pulling the sledges, he further decided that they would kill them as supplies grew lighter. The dead dogs would then be used as food for the surviving animals.

By mid December loneliness, boredom and fatigue followed them like Magi across the ice fields. Days were spent hauling sledges, digging themselves out of crevasses and constantly shouting at the dogs to keep them moving. Nights were spent in cooking, reading and sleeping.

They celebrated Christmas in a wilderness that was unending. Shackleton noted in his diary that it was a day of blinding sunshine. He produced a Christmas pudding which he had been carrying in a spare sock, and it was served hot with cocoa.

His diary for the day gave priority to food, then marching, then health and then thoughts of home.

'The warmest day we have yet had. Yet we made our best march doing over ten miles. Though we did all the pulling practically for the dogs were done up with the heat. Got up at 8.30 a.m. and B was cook. Breakfast a panikin of seal's liver and bacon with biscuit topped up with a spoonful of blackberry jam each. Then I set camera and took 2 photos of party connecting piece of rope to camera lever. Then did 4 hours march. lunch I cook. Bov Choc Plasmon biscuit 2 spoons jam each. very good. hot lunch. then two and a half hour march camp for night. I cook and in 35 min. cooked 6 pan of N.A.O.R. & biscuit for Hoosh. Boiled plum pudding and made cocoa. then we had jam to finish up so were really full for once. It is settled for our furthest South to be on 28th then we go into the land. Medical examtn. Shews Capt & I to be inclined to scurvy so will not be going on further as we are far from our base. We hope to cross 82 degrees S in 2 days anyhow. What a Christmas baking hot. It must have been so different at home.'

The men also took the opportunity to name a nearby peak Christmas Mountain, in honour of the day.

Wilson was now hoping that Scott might decide to turn for home. Scott, on the other hand, felt that the very least they must do was to reach 82 degrees south. On 28 December they achieved this goal with Shackleton, out in front, pulling the sledges in the same committed, almost manic way he had been doing for weeks. His head was constantly bent low, straining in the traces, his boots feathered in snow and ice. It was a source of pride and accomplishment to him that he was the first to cross the line, another small victory over Scott. And, yet, his overpowering emotion was one of disappointment.

All along, Shackleton had seen this expedition as an attack on the Pole. The scientific experiments and the farthest south achievements were not the object of the exercise. Neither glorious failure nor the humiliation of a badly organized fiasco held any appeal. He had wanted, more than anything, to be part of the campaign. The personal friction between Scott and himself was an element of the price to be paid for that privilege, but the fact that they might not make a serious attempt on the Pole had never been a real consideration. Now, as the pace slowed and the reality of the party's desperation set in, he knew that this was a journey that would end in defeat.

Wilson's worry, meanwhile, deepened. All three men were showing definite and recurring signs of scurvy. Wilson was anxious to turn for *Discovery*. The notion of defeat, however, was also weighing on Scott. He had come south with the hopes of Britain on his shoulders. The achievement of the South Pole was no longer a real possibility but that of getting farthest south was, and he determined to continue until that goal had been achieved.

On 30 December this objective was attained when the three reached 82 degrees 15' – they had become the first men to travel this far south. That afternoon, leaving Shackleton to guard the camp – against what no one knew – Scott and Wilson pushed on to 82 degrees 17'. Whether Scott's decision to leave Shackleton behind was one of mercy – allowing him to rest – or one of jealousy – not wanting him to be part of the farthest south achievement – remains uncertain. What Scott and Wilson did do was to name an inlet at the new farthest south point after Shackleton. But all of this, naming new points, travelling two hundred miles farther than any previous explorers, prospecting new coastline, was hollow stuff. The South Pole remained as elusive as it had done when they left England.

The three turned north as the New Year broke, with just over two weeks to reach the nearest food depot, still a hundred miles away. The remaining dogs were becoming less and less useful, and the burden of responsibility and disappointment was weighing more heavily on Scott.

Now only five of the nineteen dogs remained and the men were doing all of the work in pulling the sledges. If science was important to the captain, getting back safely to *Discovery* was uppermost in Wilson and Shackleton's minds.

As they trudged northward, Wilson noticed that Shackleton was constantly short of breath and they were forced to allow for extra stops. When he was capable of walking, his pace had slowed considerably. Again, Scott was forced to make an important decision. Rations, which were rapidly running out, would be cut again, otherwise the reduced pace might see them short of the food depot without supplies.

The depot flag, when they saw it, was glimpsed by accident. Nevertheless, the fresh supplies allowed them their first decent meals in many days. Even this improvement in diet didn't seem to help Shackleton. His cough had worsened and he was hacking blood. Scott forbade him to pull the sledges. The man who had previously been the mainstay of this work was forced to walk behind, still wearing his harness, while his companions laboured through the snow. On 18 January he collapsed with chest pains.

While the collapse itself was unexpected, Shackleton's health had been a constant source of worry to Wilson. He had not undergone any serious medical examination before joining the expedition and, since their arrival in Antarctica he'd had a series of illnesses. During the early training expeditions, he had suffered from stiffness and then a worrying cough, that had reappeared as soon as the push south had begun. It was clear that Shackleton was not a well man.

Scott and Wilson knew they couldn't carry Shackleton. There were only two dogs remaining, neither of them properly trained. There was nothing for it but to continue walking.

Again, Shackleton tried to ski but was hardly likely, in bad health, to master a skill he'd failed to learn in good health. When he used them, they were little more than large shoes.

The men came up with another device, which did help. They made a sail and mounted it on the front sledge, the wind catching it and moving the sledge, and the following sledges, along. But the sledges were now moving too fast for the men to keep up. Shackleton was put on the end sledge and given the job of using the brake to slow the train's progress. In his condition, however, he was too weak to do even this and, instead, Scott and Wilson travelled alongside the sledges, keeping them in check, while Shackleton walked behind, alone and at his own pace.

Shackleton's ill-health became a flashpoint between Scott and Wilson. Scott regularly referred to Shackleton as a 'lame duck' and an 'invalid'. This greatly angered Wilson who, when Shackleton was out of hearing, berated Scott for his insensitivity.

As January ebbed Wilson became concerned that Shackleton was more seriously ill than he had thought. On the night of 29 January a feverish Shackleton overheard Wilson tell Scott that he didn't expect him to survive until morning. Whether the thought of death galvanized him towards recovery or whether the worst of the sickness had passed, Shackleton was able to leave the tent the following day with the help of the other two. For a time he

On 3 February 1903, left to right, Shackleton, Scott and Wilson – after the southern journey.

laboured along on his skis but after a couple of hours even this proved impossible and he was put sitting in one of the sledges. By mid-afternoon he felt well enough to get back on the skis. Scott found it difficult to contain his annoyance. Energy that might have gone into sketching and notation was being used in looking after Shackleton.

Fortunately, on 3 February, six miles from *Discovery*, the three were met by Louis Bernacchi and Reginald Skelton, who took over the pulling of the sledges. At the ship there was flag-waving, cheering, songs and the warmest of welcomes. For Shackleton there must have been echoes of the welcomes his sisters had organized for him in London. This time, however, he had neither the strength nor inclination to object or enjoy. While the music and drinking went on into the small hours, he had a bath and retired to his bunk.

As Scott, Wilson and Shackleton were making their way back to the ship, the relief vessel *Morning* arrived. With *Discovery* due to spend another year in Antarctica, *Morning* had been sent to renew supplies and take home those who were not staying for another winter.

Scott asked Dr Reginald Koettlitz, senior surgeon on *Discovery*, to examine Shackleton. Koettlitz informed Scott that Shackleton had almost completely recovered from the effects of the trip. Scott wasn't convinced. He believed Shackleton had hidden the signs of illness before setting out on the expedition and that he was not sufficiently well to warrant his continuing on the *Discovery*. He informed Shackleton that he was being invalided home.

On the last evening of February 1903 Shackleton's companions sent him on his way with a dinner. The following day, carrying his luggage, he walked across the ice to the waiting relief ship. That night he wrote in his diary:

'*A beautiful day, but a sad one indeed for me: for today I left my home and all those who are chums as much as I ever will have any one for chums. I cannot write about it but it touched me more than I can say when the men came up on deck and gave me 3 parting cheers. Ah. It was hard to have to leave before the work is over and especially to leave those who will have to stay down here in the cold dark days for there seems to my mind but little chance of the old ship going out: Michael Ferrar came along with me and I went slowly for I had only been twice out of the ship since I came back from the southern journey. We had a very pleasant evening on "Morning" and with songs and one thing and another it was 3 am before we went to bed.*'

As *Morning* set sail, snow was falling and then the sun came out and Shackleton stood on deck, watching his hopes and aspirations fade behind him. When, finally, he went to his cabin he tried to read but, as he wrote, his thoughts went back: 'I took the photos of all our chaps before starting so that our people at home may have the last glimpse of their faces should we not succeed in getting out or they not succeed, I mean.'

Among the men to whom he refers were Wilson, his good friend, and Scott, the man who would become his arch-rival, though this was a rivalry that lay ahead. For now there was disappointment but also the novelty of being the first to return with an account of the adventure.

In Christchurch Shackleton awaited a passage home, and organized stores for *Morning*, which was to return as a relief ship to *Discovery*. Finally, on 9 May, he left New Zealand and sailed via San Francisco and New York on the *Orotava*. As he wrote in his diary, he was 'really going home'. He also made some caustic notes on his travelling companions:

'There are a fair number of passengers on board but they seem to be a pretty dull and uninteresting crowd. There is one individual or rather two that I have made up my mind not to sit near for coming up in the train they did nothing but growl and talk about their aches "More!! More!! About yourself!!!" You know the type and very fussy reddish grey beard man and a fat and unwieldy woman they instinctively repel one even before you say a word to them and I do not intend to ...'

On the homeward journey he had plenty of time to sieve through the memories and experiences of Antarctica. By the time he reached London, on 15 June, he resolved to return to the southern continent, but this time as leader of his own expedition.

5

Shackleton at Home

1903–1907

---◆---

Shackleton's return to England was brightened by the prospect of seeing Emily again. Their meeting, on 12 June, was emotional. She had received letters from Shackleton, telling her he was recovered from the ordeal of 'breaking down', but she can hardly have expected to meet a man who was rested, sun-tanned and, apparently, in fine physical health.

Shackleton was disappointed not to have completed the Antarctic expedition. But he was heartened by the warm welcome from Sir Clements Markham, who wrote: 'I admire your pluck and the way you held out, and everyone speaks with admiration of it and of their sincere friendship for you.' Better still, Shackleton embarked on a round of lectures aimed at finding extra funds for the expedition. Most importantly, being the first man back, he enjoyed the kudos of telling the story of the expedition to date.

But Markham had other reasons for wanting Shackleton on side. There was much unhappiness in British geographical circles about *Discovery* spending an unanticipated second winter in the Antarctic. Markham, the target of criticism for what was now a financial disaster, met Shackleton the morning after his arrival in London, who agreed to do what he could to ease the situation.

In practical ways he was also able to help his colleagues still in Antarctica. Firstly, he advised on the equipping of the *Terra Nova*, a relief ship being fitted out by the Royal Navy to assist the *Discovery*. Secondly, he was asked to help fit out the *Uruguay*, a relief ship organized by the Argentinian government to rescue Nordenskjold's Swedish expedition, after the loss of their ship the *Antartctic* in the Weddell Sea area. He was also invited to serve as an officer on the *Terra Nova*, an invitation he declined.

In June Shackleton wrote articles for supplements in the *Illustrated London News*, giving his account of the first year of the expedition. In the articles, he referred to the fact that he 'broke down owing to overstrain ... I was, however, able to march the nine or ten miles a day that the party made ... Captain Scott and Dr Wilson could not have done more for me than they did. They were bearing the brunt of the work.'

The following month, he applied for a position as supplementary Lieutenant in the Royal Navy. The main reason for his application was to give him a steady income which would allow him to marry Emily. While she had an allowance of £700 a year for life, from her father's will, Shackleton was adamant that he must provide for her himself.

Markham, on behalf of the Royal Geographical Society and its President, William Huggins, recommended Shackleton for the position but the naval list was closed and the application was unsuccessful – which left Shackleton with the problem of no job, no income and no immediate prospects of marriage.

Meanwhile, fundraising and publicity for the *Discovery* expedition continued. In September he gave a slide lecture at a British Association meeting in Southport, earning praise for intriguing the audience without stealing Scott's thunder before his return.

Autumn saw Shackleton take a job as a sub-editor on the *Royal Magazine*. His experience on various naval and expeditionary magazines and papers had given him the idea that journalism might be for him. He was hardly qualified, however, and ended up enquiring of the editor how to correct a proof. Untroubled by his ignorance, he simply got on with entertaining office colleagues with tales of his Antarctic adventure.

In November he was invited to lecture to the Royal Scottish Geographical Society, speaking in Edinburgh on the 11th, Glasgow on the 14th and Aberdeen on the 15th. While there, he discovered that the position of secretary to the RSGS was about to become vacant and that it carried a salary. His pending marriage to Emily – fixed for the following spring – made the position all the more attractive. On 4 December he applied for the job with the backing of several notable members of the Geographical Society in England and the commendations of Markham and Huggins.

Huggins praised Shackleton's 'enthusiasm for geographical exploration'; Markham wrote that he believed he would be 'invaluable in the work of increasing the number of members' and Hugh Robert Mill described him as a man 'keen in taking up a new train of thought or line of work, and persevering'.

J. Scott Keltie, Secretary of the Royal Geographical Society wrote that he thought 'the Society would be fortunate in obtaining [Shackleton's] services'.

Shackleton felt confident about his chances but reckoned without the entrenched ideas of the Society committee, who noted two grammatical errors in his letter of application. He also heard that there were 'many men with splendid qualifications against me'.

14 South Learmonth Gardens, Edinburgh, Scotland. Shackleton and Emily lived here from April 1904 to 1907, paying £125 a year rent whilst he worked for the Scottish RGS. Now part of Channings Hotel.

Mill was quick to reassure him, writing: '… if you are not appointed Secretary of the R.S.G.S. I will resign my membership of that Society and take no more interest in its affairs to the end of time … I know you are the best man for the job and a great deal too good for it too.'

On Christmas Eve a meeting of the Society failed to reach a decision, with members split between Shackleton and a candidate called Johnstone. Fortunately for Shackleton, one of his advocates, J.G. Bartholomew, had the vote postponed.

On 11 January, with Shackleton's supporters returned from their Christmas holidays, he was unanimously elected.

With a job that offered a regular income, Shackleton and Emily could now concentrate on their wedding. It would be necessary for Emily to move to Scotland and Shackleton, who intially stayed with the Beardmore family, set about finding a house. This he did, at 14

*Emily Mary
Shackleton, née
Dorman (1868-1936),
daughter of Charles
Dorman and Jane née
Swinford. Emily
married Shackleton at
Christ Church
Westminster on 9
April 1904.*

South Learmonth Gardens, on the edge of Edinburgh. The house was small but sufficient and approved by Emily.

Shackleton believed the honeymoon should be postponed until he was well settled in his new job. He wrote to Emily, using his most persuasive tone: 'I think we would be happier in our own little home … there is sunshine here too and there will be sunshine in our lives … It would be such a rush … and here we would be so quiet and I could take you away for a month in Sept or August or whenever you like.'

Emily, not for the last time, conceded to his wish.

Shackleton threw himself into the new job, reorganizing the office, setting up a series of lectures and delivering one himself on the subject of the farthest south. His warm attitude and his willingness to, mostly, humour those whom he felt were talking 'drivel' saw membership of the Society grow from 1430 to 1832, while the attendance at lectures leapt from just over two hundred to well over sixteen hundred. Most importantly, the Society's bank balance increased from £50 to almost £350.

On 9 April 1904 Shackleton and Emily were married at Christ Church, Westminister. Cyril Longhurst was his best man. The wedding breakfast was eaten in Sir Clements Markham's home in Eccleston Square. Markham had been invited to the wedding but was too ill to attend so breakfasting with him was, in Shackleton's eyes, a sign of friendship and loyalty. Immediately afterwards, the newly weds returned to Edinburgh and work with renewed energy. Without doubt Shackleton was happy with his new bride. She was the beautiful older woman he had been chasing for years. Emily, for her part, made every effort to immerse herself in the Edinburgh social circle.

A letter, sent to Emily with roses on her birthday, 15 May, is full of love and passion from the absent Shackleton who was away on business:

> *My darling Sweeteyes and wife.*
>
> *Just a bunch of roses from your husband and lover forever and ever. I can see you darling reading this in bed today and am longing to be beside you in my own place. I am coming back quickly to you dear heart so do not be sad. I will be wanting you sorely today dearest. I hope the roses will be sweet.*
>
> *The loveliest birthday wishes to my darling from her husband.*

Shackleton thrived in this new milieu, making himself a sought-after guest, renowned for his stories, wit and charm. He and Emily entertained regularly and quickly made many new friends, among them the statesman, Lord Rosebery, the scientist, Professor Crum Brown, and the captain of industry, William Beardmore.

Shackleton frequently travelled to London on Society business and it was there, in the summer of 1904, that he read the letters, from *Discovery*, by then in New Zealand, announcing that Scott and his colleagues would soon be back in England. Shackleton would have to make way, in the public imagination, for his Captain.

In the meantime, he and Emily took their postponed honeymoon in Dornoch, where they had a golfing holiday.

On 16 September he was back in London for lunch on the deck of the *Discovery*, which had berthed at the East India Dock. In early November he attended a formal dinner of welcome at the Savage Club and received the Polar Medal, the king's award for polar exploration, and a silver medal from the Royal Geographical Society. Scott received a gold medal.

Shackleton and Emily both enjoyed golf, which they played in Dornoch during a delayed honeymoon in summer 1904. Emily was the better player. (Courtesy Rhod McEwan)

Shackleton arranged for Scott to deliver lectures to RSGS members in Edinburgh, Dundee and Glasgow, and told him that he had given up the notion of another expedition. 'There seems to be no money about and besides I am settled down now and have to make money it would only break up my life, if I could stand it which Wilson thinks I could not.'

The return of Scott and his promotion to the rank of naval captain, the public interest in him and his achievements, all cast a deep gloom over Shackleton and it was obvious that he was finding life in Scott's shadow trying.

On 12 November Scott was guest of honour at the Scottish Society banquet and Markham travelled north for the occasion. During the visit he warned Emily that Shackleton was 'doing much more than the work of one man'.

Shackleton, however, didn't consider himself overburdened. On a visit to London in November he called to the Liberal Unionist Council and met Sir John Boraston, the chief Liberal Unionist agent, who suggested he might consider standing as a candidate in Dundee.

The Liberal Unionists were a breakaway group, having split from the Liberal Party in 1886, when the latter espoused Home Rule for Ireland. The dissenters, led by Joseph Chamberlain, established the new party and allied themselves with the Conservative Party.

It was ironic that they should be pursuing an Irishman as their candidate for Dundee, and even more so that the young boy with the strong Irish accent should now be a man willing to stand against Home Rule for his own country.

There are two aspects to this, neither of which reflects well on Shackleton. On the one hand, he may have felt that Ireland did not merit self-rule. If so, he showed little faith in his fellow countrymen – nor, by extension, in the people of Scotland. If, on the other hand, the candidacy was simply a step up a personal social ladder, it was an unconsidered one, dismissing the genuine aspirations of a people for personal gain. As with his decision to become a Freemason, there was no question which side of his family history was the more influential.

The Liberals had a reasonably safe seat in Dundee but the Liberal Unionists persuaded Shackleton that he had a fighting chance of taking it for them and this was enough to win his agreement. The Dundee Liberal Unionist committee, in its haste to parade the new boy, announced his candidacy before he had been approved by the general committee of the party and before he had time to tell his employers at the RSGS. Mundane as his work had become, he hadn't been prepared to step down as Secretary without alternative employment in sight. Now, it appeared, his new-found friends in the Liberal Unionist Party had fouled him up on two fronts.

Hugh Robert Mill was highly critical of Shackleton, on political and personal grounds, and Shackleton found himself defending his decision.

'I am perfectly honest,' he wrote to Mill, 'and it is not from any idea of newspaper publicity I became connected with politics, but as the result of careful thought on my part and a conviction that what I uphold is right.'

His claims to probity don't quite ring true. Shackleton wasn't particularly political and his knowledge of national and international affairs was no deeper than average. Protest as he might, his candidacy lacked conviction.

In early January 1905 he offered his resignation as Secretary of the RSGS. Two months later the Society, while 'deeply regretting' his candidacy for parliament, postponed its acceptance of his resignation. Shackleton, however, insisted that he was leaving. July was agreed as a parting date.

This left Shackleton with the recurring problem of finding a job. He talked to William Beardmore, a businessman with a shipbuilding firm on the Clyde, who promised to find him work. The birth of the Shackletons' first child, Raymond, on 2 February, came as a reminder that a career and a steady income were part and parcel of being a family man.

In April Shackleton travelled to Glasgow and had further discussions with Beardmore. He wrote, optimistic as ever, to Emily telling her there were 'four separate things that I can go into ... He [Beardmore] tells me that I can only begin at £300 but that the beginning is nothing if I do what he wishes and show I can work ... He is the sort of man who would raise me another £300 if he thinks I am doing well.'

Apart from shipbuilding, Beardmore had just bought out the Arrol-Johnston Motor Works and thought Shackleton would be useful in this company. Beardmore's wife Elspeth, whose interest in Shackleton was as much personal as professional, believed he could become an assistant to her husband. As was so often the case in Shackleton's career, nothing specific was decided beyond the promise of a job, should Shackleton fail to be elected.

Shackleton made other plans for garnering money. One was the opening of a shop and office to promote Tabard cigarettes. Several of his friends invested in the project, which was moderately successful but never likely to make his fortune.

That summer Shackleton, in company with Dr Charles Sarolea, the fiancé of Emily's sister Julia, visited the continent. The pair had hit on the idea of establishing an international news agency. Shackleton sank £500 into the venture and there was talk of introductions to royal circles in Belgium. The news agency was to be called Potentia. It may have been optimistically named but it proved even less successful than the cigarette company and, despite much talk, never got off the ground.

As the summer ended Shackleton's mind turned more and more to the notion of raising funds for another Antarctic expedition. This had been in his head since his return from the *Discovery* trip but now, with his boredom threshold falling, he became more convinced that it was something he must do. Scott's high profile in the public mind was a reminder of his own apparent failure. Most tellingly, in a lecture given by Scott in November – and widely reported in the newspapers – he had mentioned that he and Wilson had had to 'draw the sledge with their comrade who had become ill'. He felt humiliated at the thought of people knowing he had been unable to walk all the way, and Scott's reference to the fact angered him greatly. This, combined with Scott's less than flattering account of Shackleton's breakdown in his newly published *The Voyage of the 'Discovery'* seem to have been the spark that rekindled his commitment to going south again and proving he was every bit the man Scott was.

What angered Shackleton most was Scott's failure to mention his steering the sledge while riding on it. Furthermore, in describing the condition of each of the three after their return to *Discovery* Scott claimed that he was by far the fittest, and that Shackleton 'would creep into his cabin and … rest until the exertion had worn off'.

That so much rested on so little says much about the competition between the pair. Scott had his doubts about Shackleton and felt the merchant seaman didn't respect him as he might have done. Shackleton was more convinced than ever that the Royal Navy man was jealous and would do him down at every opportunity.

The calling of an election in December turned Shackleton's attention temporarily to the imminent campaign. As with all things bright and new, he immersed himself in the business of politics, addressing up to six meetings each day and mingling freely with the electorate. He promoted himself as a working man who had earned his living with his hands, and he throve on the rough and tumble of the hustings. Such was the warmth of the welcome he received in some parts of Dundee that he believed himself to have 'a good chance' of being elected. He also argued that, in standing against Home Rule for Ireland, he was a 'true patriot' who believed in King and Empire, an unwelcome line of reasoning in some parts of the city where the bulk of the population comprised Irish emigrants.

In working-class areas he played the anti-German card, blaming Britain's industrial troubles on German government subsidies for their manufacturers. In other company he pushed the idea of a stronger British empire through reinforced links between Britain and Ireland. When the election was held on 16 January 1906, Shackleton finished fourth of five in the poll. He may have got the cheers but the votes were another matter and the seats went to a Liberal and a Labour Party candidate. Times were changing and the Labour movement was on the rise.

No sooner was the election over, however, than Shackleton was in London involved in another money-making venture to ship Russian troops back home from the Far East.

Frank, Ernest's younger brother, Dublin Herald at the Office of Arms, who resigned in November 1907 following the disappearance in July of the insignia of the Grand Master and five gold collars of the Order of St Patrick.

Right: Shackleton coat of arms. In 1898 Sir Arthur Vicars, Ulster King of Arms, confirmed the use of arms to Joseph Fisher Shackleton of Lucan, County Dublin, and his grandfather Abraham of Ballitore and their descendants. Frank had printed a family tree to show his family's descent from Louis VIII King of France and King John of England and, through the Fitzmaurices, to the barons of Kerry, the earls of Ormonde and King Edward I of England among others.

Shackleton.

According to a letter sent to Emily, the Russians were going to pay '£12 per head for the soldiers and £40 for each officer … and we could clear £100,000 but I cannot go into details now: and I don't want to raise hopes'. And rightly so. On 9 February he wrote that 'things will be alright'. By 14 February '6500 troops have been signed for by contract which will receive official rectification tomorrow'.

But another great plan disappeared, the contract didn't come through, and the project was abandoned. Shackleton returned to Scotland and a job with Beardmore's company.

Again, he was optimistic. He wrote to Emily: 'Will has given me a room right opposite his own so I am to be in close touch with him … I mean to do my very best in this matter as he says his trouble is with me not having initiative enough.'

Nothing less than a directorship in his new employer's company was in his sights. The fact that his younger brother, Frank, was progressing in society was another reminder that he was not making headway as quickly as he might have imagined.

In 1899 Frank had found a job, through friends, with the Office of Arms in Dublin. After a sojourn in the army during the Boer War, he returned to Dublin and by 1903 was a Gold Staff Officer in the Heraldry Office in Dublin Castle. By 1905 he had advanced to the position of Dublin Herald. He had also managed to find himself three homes, in London, Devon and Dublin.

Ernest, meanwhile, was commuting daily from Edinburgh to Glasgow. Beardmore appointed him as secretary to a committee established to investigate the design of a new gas engine. Shackleton was note-taker to a panel of gas experts. Afterwards, he rewrote the notes and sent them for typing. He also travelled regularly to London on company business, interviewing prospective clients.

While in London he pursued a friendship with an American living there, a Miss Havemeyer. Whether this was a sexual relationship is unclear but Emily found the business of pregnancy 'distasteful' and Shackleton was said to have been 'virtually driven' to find sexual satisfaction outside his marriage. What is clear is that the time spent there was more interesting than the time spent in William Beardmore's office. The jobs given to Shackleton were time-consuming but boredom was setting in again. Closer to home, his friendship with Elspeth Beardmore too was deepening, and he claimed he always felt the more cheerful for meeting her.

Other problems were a constant drain on his financial and mental resources. His father was no longer practising full-time and needed money. His sisters also needed regular support and, in his own home, Raymond was ill and Emily was finding her second pregnancy no easier than her first. Elspeth Beardmore, at least, was not only sympathetic but encouraging as Shackleton became increasingly convinced that his best chance of security lay to the south.

The South Pole still awaited its first visitors and the call was growing louder. The Antarctic was a place he knew, where he could be his own man. It was also a potential gold-mine, if only he could find the initial capital to exploit it.

In searching for financial backers Shackleton put together a proposal for another expedition. This included the use of dogs, sledges and a 'specially designed motor car'.

Furthermore, he wrote, 'with sixty dogs and a couple of ponies, I am quite certain that the South Pole could be reached'.

Part of the plan was to have the car pull ten sledges, one of which would be dropped every hundred miles as a depot. Not only that but, travelling fifty miles a day in the car he believed he might be able to go 'beyond the South Pole and branch off East and West'. A second party would travel to the magnetic pole, without the assistance of the car. The expeditionary force would make use of the hut left by the crew of the *Discovery*. He estimated the cost of this expedition at £17,000.

Two days before Christmas Shackleton's plans were put on hold by the birth of his first daughter, Cecily. Over the Christmas holiday, while his wife recovered, Shackleton refocused on his expedition.

What he didn't explain were his reasons for wanting to go. There were many. He needed to prove himself to himself following his illness on the Scott expedition; he wished to prove himself to his wife; he wanted to make money; he needed excitement; he wanted fame and he was committed to geographical and scientific exploration and achievement. Reaching the South Pole would resolve everything.

To add to his worries, there were rumours that the Frenchman Charcot and the Belgian Arctowski were planning an expedition to the Antarctic. Shackleton redoubled his efforts and got some promises of money. Elizabeth Dawson-Lambton donated £1000 which Ernest passed to his brother Frank to invest while the expedition plans were developed. Frank's notion of investment was to use the money to bail out one of his own companies.

Travelling to London when he could, Shackleton continued his fundraising drive. Douglas Spens Steuart, a mining engineer who had just established a company called Celtic Investment Trust, agreed to allow 10,000 shares in the company to be used as backing for the expedition. The dream seemed achievable.

On a more practical level, Shackleton was faced with the problem of telling William Beardmore that he wanted leave to travel to the Antarctic again, having assured Beardmore only a year before that he had given up all ideas of another expedition. To Shackleton's delight, not only did Beardmore agree to let him go, he also agreed to go guarantor for some of the finances for the trip.

On 11 February, at a dinner hosted by the Royal Geographical Society in London, both Shackleton and Arctowski formally outlined their plans for expeditions to the South Pole. The following day's newspapers brought the news to the public. A month later, Shackleton published a detailed account: 'I do not intend to sacrifice the scientific utility of the expedition,' he wrote, 'to a mere record-breaking journey, but say frankly, all the same, that one of my great efforts will be to reach the southern geographical pole.'

There were other changes from the plans of the year before. The expedition party would be larger; the ship to take them south would be bought rather than specifically built; she would drop the expeditionary force and then journey back to New Zealand, returning the following year as a relief vessel. The party heading for the magnetic pole would be landed separately, ideally in Victoria Land, close to their course southward.

Shackleton concluded his proposal with a résumé of the aims: 'By the southern and eastern sledge journey we may possibly solve the problem of the great ice-barrier ... by the charting of new mountains and discovery of new lands in the far south we aid geographical science; by the magnetic work we help not only the academic side of magnetic science, but we may help the mercantile community in the way of better ... charts.'

The ultimate financing of the trip was to be made by selling shares from Celtic Investment to anyone willing to buy them. In turn, when he got back, he would repay his debts by writing a book, lecturing and writing for newspapers. Not only did he believe he could repay these debts, he believed that long sought-after fortune lay at the end of this particular expedition.

He wrote to Emily: 'the book ... means £10,000 if we are successful and that is quite apart from all newspaper news ... so it will leave me all the lectures etc free and the book can pay off the guarantees if people really want them ... I think it will be worth about £30,000 in the way of lectures alone ... Then Sweetheart we will settle down to a quiet life.'

With finances potentially under control, Shackleton set about organizing a crew. Among those he contacted was George Mulock – the man who had replaced him on the *Discovery*. He was shocked to learn, when Mulock replied, that he had committed himself to travelling south on another expedition, one about which Shackleton knew nothing, led by Scott.

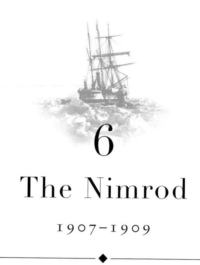

6

The Nimrod

1907–1909

---◆---

Shackleton wrote, in the opening chapter of *The Heart of the Antarctic*, his memoir of the 1907-1909 British expedition: 'Men go into the void spaces of the world for various reasons. Some are actuated simply by a love of adventure, some have the keen thirst for scientific knowledge, and others again are drawn away from the trodden paths by "the lure of little voices," the mysterious fascination of the unknown. I think that in my own case it was a combination of these factors that determined me to try my fortune once again in the frozen south.'

What he didn't say was that failure was a sharp spur. Combining with his passionate desire to be back on the Antarctic ice, it drove him to organize the *Nimrod* expedition.

He also had an urge to explain the lure of the wild: 'The stark polar lands grip the hearts of the men who have lived on them in a manner that can hardly be understood by the people who have never got outside the pale of civilization.'

The Antarctic offered Shackleton a second chance to prove himself. Civilization stood for the warmth of home, of his wife and children, but it also signified the constraints of a society that knew nothing of the stimulation that danger and comradeship offered. Civilization meant making a living and supporting an extended family. Life in the civilized world was several vital steps removed from life in the wasteland.

The Antarctic held its own kinds of tensions, life lived literally on the edge; but it offered the imperative of dealing with those tensions in an immediate and physical way. When problems occurred, solutions had to be found. You solved or you died.

Returning from the *Discovery* expedition, Shackleton recognized something important had gone out of his life. This, and the gnawing suspicion that things might have gone otherwise had he not been with Scott, was the source of a deep and troubling frustration.

Later, he would tell his sister Kathleen: 'I don't want to race anyone but you can't think what it is like to walk over places where no one has ever been before.'

Raymond and Cecily, EHS's children, at Torquay, August 1907. Raymond is wrapped in the Union flag presented to EHS by Queen Alexendra.

The very people at the warm heart of Shackleton's *civilized* life, his wife, his young children, his extended family, were those who had to be considered when it came to deciding on another expedition. His elderly father and impecunious sisters; his two children under the age of two: it was hardly the best time to consider a long period of separation. However, Ernest argued that a successful journey to the South Pole would bring in enough money to make them comfortable.

At the same time, Shackleton's relationship with Elspeth Beardmore was a talking-point to many who knew them. He would write to her about his financial and family problems and then finish a letter with, 'You looked so beautiful the other night.' In his search for backing for his planned trip, she was on his mind: 'I have been hoping for a line from you.' Many, including her husband's work colleagues, suspected she was Shackleton's mistress.

Whatever the relationship, it was Elspeth who encouraged him to fulfill his dream.

Emily, suffering from post-natal depression, was less enthusiastic but recognized her husband's frustration. Ernest's going meant an absence of three years. More importantly, she would be raising the children, running their home, dealing with the demands of day-to-day survival and coming to terms with the emotional stress of parting from her husband. When finally she agreed, it was without eagerness, but once the decision was made she was committed in her support.

A letter from her sister Daisy, dated 14 February 1907, is full of sympathy and encouragement: 'I do think you are being most awfully good and brave over it all but after all it is a splendid thing to do and I think dear old Mike [Shackleton] would always have felt his life's work had been left undone if he had failed after all his trouble. I am glad for his sake he has got the money … I wondered … how you were feeling and if you were awake with a horrid sinking in your heart. I can't bear to think of Mike's going away, he is so bright and cheerie and we shall all miss him so but I cannot help thinking he has to be confident of success or he would not attempt it.'

In February 1907 Shackleton made public his expedition plans. Some queried his suitability, raising the issue of his ill health on the *Discovery* trip. Scott saw Shackleton's proposal as being in direct competition with his own long-term plan. And some, unsurprisingly, were shocked that a mere Merchant Navy upstart would dare undertake an expedition that was above his station. But such opposition and the practicalities of a lack of money were not to stand in Shackleton's way. He was committed to the expedition and to doing things on his own terms.

'*I decided I would have no committee* [he wrote] *as the expedition was entirely my own venture. I was fortunate in not being hampered by committees of any sort. I kept the control of all the arrangements in my own hands and this avoided the delays that are inevitable when a group of men have to arrive at a discussion on points of detail.*'

Shackleton approached the Royal Geographical Society for backing but he was also busy elsewhere trying to raise the necessary funds. He had already persuaded the Scottish businessman Douglas Spens Steuart, a mining engineer and partner in a firm of consultants, to back his proposal. Elspeth Beardmore helped to win financial support from her husband William, who agreed to guarantee a bank loan of £7000, on the condition that the first profitable returns from the expedition would go towards its repayment. He also insisted that the expedition ship would be his property, on loan to Shackleton for the duration of the voyage.

Beardmore was not alone in believing that Shackleton and Elspeth were involved in a long-running affair and, with Shackleton in the Antarctic, the relationship would, at the very least, be put on ice for three years.

With the promise of finance, Shackleton went to Norway to order sledges, boots, mits, sleeping-bags and skis. While there, he visited Sandefjord in the hope of agreeing a price for the 700-tonne *Bjorn*, a ship built in Dundee in Scotland specifically for polar work. The *Bjorn*, with triple-expansion engines, was ideal for the trip but its price was out of Shackleton's reach. Instead, on his return to London, he bought the *Nimrod*.

The *Nimrod*, at that time, was on a sealing expedition and was inspected on Shackleton's behalf. In mid-June she arrived on the Thames and he went to survey her. He came away from the inspection greatly disturbed.

BRITISH ANTARCTIC EXPEDITION 1907.
9 REGENT STREET, WATERLOO PLACE,
LONDON, S.W.

Part of a letter from EHS to Elspeth Beardmore, wife of William Beardmore (later Lord Invernairn), an old Dulwich boy, whom Shackleton worked for in 1906 at his Parkhead Works in Glasgow. Beardmore became a major sponsor of the Nimrod expedition whilst Shackleton became very close friends with his wife.

'She was much dilapidated and smelt strongly of seal-oil, and an inspection in dock showed that she required caulking and that her masts would have to be renewed. She was rigged only as a schooner and her masts were decayed, and I wanted to be able to sail her in the event of the engine breaking down or the supply of coal running short.'

He handed the ship to R. & H. Green of Blackhall for overhaul and, as he was later to admit, 'I had not then become acquainted with the many good qualities of the *Nimrod* and my first impression hardly did justice to the plucky old ship.'

While the vessel was being renovated, Shackleton was in negotiation with the Royal Geographical Society and Scott – often through intermediaries, notably Edward Wilson.

At the same time he pursued further patronage. The agreement of the Marquis of Graham to become a backer proved an enormous boost. With Steuart, Beardmore and Graham behind him, the way was clearing.

However, Scott was now making demands on Shackleton about where he might land and where he might travel. Scott the explorer had suddenly become Scott the dog in the Antarctic manger.

Shackleton wasn't the only one receiving this treatment from the British geographic establishment at the time. The Polish scientist and explorer Henryk Arctowski was treated with imperial disdain by Sir Clements Markham. Arctowski's plan was similar to Shackleton's and the object of even greater arrogance. 'I certainly should have been much annoyed', Markham wrote, 'if that fellow Arctowski had gone poaching down in our preserves; but I believe he has not got any funds. Foreigners never get much beyond the Antarctic circle.'

Shackleton's initial reaction to Scott was to compromise. In spite of their differences, he didn't believe he should offend the man with whom he had sailed. But as the demands grew more specific, Shackleton reached a point of barely concealed exasperation in a letter to Scott in March 1907:

'I have been ready, as you realize, to meet you as regards McMurdo Base. I realize myself what I have given up in regard to this matter. Concerning the 170 Meridian West as a line of demarkation [sic], this matter will have to be discussed. I must tell you quite frankly that my agreement to this proposition might perhaps make a position untenable to me on my Southward Journey and that I do not see my way, at the present moment, to accede to this. I also consider that the unknown land or the disputed land of Wilkes is free to anybody who wishes to explore that part, and as you know, my programme originally included the exploration of this quarter.

I am ready to discuss with you the whole matter but I want you to understand that I do not look upon either Wood Bay or the land to the West of Cape North as being within the Province of any particular previous expedition. As you write to me openly, I therefore answer you in the same manner.'

Letters continued to be exchanged until, in April, the two men met. Shackleton set out the specifics that had been agreed. The list was long, and detailed the areas Shackleton would and would not traverse.

In May Shackleton forwarded the plan to Scott, whose response was as amenable and businesslike as it had previously been parsimonious:

My dear Shackleton,

I return you this copy of your letter which is a very clear statement of the arrangement to which we came. If as you say you will rigidly adhere to it, I do not think our plans will clash and I shall feel on sure ground in developing my own.

Yours very sincerely R.F. Scott.

In spite of all the pressures, Shackleton continued to immerse himself in the preparations. The *Discovery* trip had taught him the importance of groundwork: 'The equipping of a Polar expedition is a task demanding experience as well as the greatest attention to points of detail. When the expedition has left civilization there is no opportunity to repair any omission or secure any article that may have been forgotten.'

Most important in the preparations was the listing of possible crew-members for the expedition. He was extremely anxious that Edward Wilson, one of the intermediaries between Scott and himself, should accompany him. Wilson was a doctor and Shackleton believed he'd be an invaluable asset, both as a medical practitioner and as a colleague. Wilson, however, caught between loyalty to Scott and Shackleton, used the fact that he was busy conducting a survey of grouse disease in Scotland as an excuse not to travel. Despite intense pressure, he flatly refused to join the expedition.

Meanwhile, equipment for the trip was being prepared. A typewriter, a sewing-machine, a gramophone, a printing-press, hockey sticks and a football were among the less obvious but important items for inclusion, but by far the most intriguing was a 15-horsepower Arrol-Johnston car. Shackleton explained his decision subsequently.

*Shackleton's hut
at Cape Royds, on
Ross Island. Fifteen
men overwintered
in this. The hut is
still there.*

'I decided to take a motor-car because I thought it possible, from my previous experience, that we might meet with a hard surface on the great ice Barrier, over which the first part, at any rate, on the journey towards the south would have to be performed. On a reasonably good surface the machine would be able to haul a heavy load at a rapid pace.'

Taking the car on the trip was good for publicity but proved impractical, its two-ton weight quickly bogged down in the soft snow. Of far greater use were the ten Manchurian ponies which were to join the ship in New Zealand. These had been taken from a wild herd of over 2000 ponies in Tientsin. Also due for collection in New Zealand were nine Siberian dogs, veterans of a previous expedition.

In Norway Shackleton had ordered sledges, designed by the Norwegian explorer Fridtjof Nansen, and reindeer-skin sleeping-bags. He also bought eighty pairs of dog- and wolf-skin mits and eighty pairs of finnesko boots made from the skin of reindeer head. Fifty kilos of Sennegrass was brought to absorb the sweat from feet in the boots.

For shelter, a pre-fabricated hut made by Humphrey's of Knightsbridge, and measuring 33'x 19'x 8' was included with the equipment. The roof and walls of the hut were covered in felt and the walls were made of 1" boards with 4" cavities filled with granulated cork for insulation. The hut was divided into cubicles with two men sharing an area of 7'x 9'x 1'5". Acetylene gas was used for lighting and an anthracite stove for heating and cooking.

Food was an essential and Shackleton had strong ideas about what should and shouldn't be taken. He believed the food must be wholesome, varied, nourishing and light to carry, good for physical health and a morale booster for the men. The stores taken included treats such as fish-balls, roast reindeer and roast ptarmigan. Twenty-seven cases of Montserrat lime juice, essential against scurvy, were also included. Under the supervision of manager Alfred Reid, the stores for the trip were packed in 2500 Veneseta cases and loaded onto the *Nimrod*.

Having abandoned hope of persuading Wilson to come, Shackleton set about interviewing and selecting members of the expedition. He had definite ideas on the qualities required: 'The men selected must be qualified to work. They must be able to live together in harmony for a long period without outside communication, and it must be remembered that the men whose desires lead them to the untrodden paths of the world have generally marked individuality.'

Shackleton particularly wanted two surgeons, a biologist and a geologist in the group. From the more than 400 applicants he chose his shore party. Of those chosen, all but three were unknown to him.

Lieutenant Jameson Boyd Adams had begun his career in the Merchant, before moving to the Royal Navy. When Shackleton invited him to take a place on the expedition he had just been offered a permanent commission in the Royal Navy but he opted, instead, to travel on the *Nimrod*.

Sir Philip Brocklehurst, a nineteen-year old, shared Shackleton's passion for boxing, and spent some time studying geology and surveying to assure his place in the final party.

Raymond Priestley was a twenty-year-old geology student. His memories were that the interview with Shackleton was somewhat unusual: 'He asked me if I could sing and I said I couldn't; and he asked me if I would know gold if I saw it, and again I said No! He must have asked me other questions but I remember these because they were bizarre.'

George Marston was expedition artist and practical joker in the pack. Dr Eric Marshall was senior surgeon made responsible for photography. Alistair Forbes Mackay was second surgeon.

Bernard Day, who had worked with the Arrol-Johnston Motor-Car Company, was brought along as driver and mechanic, and hotel chef William Roberts joined as cook. Ernest Joyce was given responsibility for looking after dogs and sledges, and Bertram Armytage was to look after the ponies taken on the expedition. Frank Wild was in charge of provisions, while James Murray was principal biologist.

Later, from Australia, Professor T.W. Edgeworth David would travel as director of the scientific staff and Douglas Mawson would be taken on as a physicist.

Early in July an exhibition of some of the stores and provisions was held in a room in Regent Street. It proved to be a popular event attended by thousands of visitors coming to see the array of foodstuffs and equipment.

Finally, on 30 July 1907, the *Nimrod* left the East India docks on the first stage of her long journey to New Zealand.

On 4 August King Edward VII and Queen Alexandra visited the ship at Cowes on the Isle of Wight.

Emily recorded in her diary: 'I was greatly favoured by a special Royal permission to be on board ... The King greeted Ernest with a cheery "Ah, there you are – very pleased to see you again." It was so sweet of the Queen to give Ernest a flag ... Ernest looked his best and you would know how nice that is. I was very proud of him.'

On the same visit, Shackleton was conferred with the Victorian Order.

Three days later the *Nimrod* sailed from Torquay, arriving in New Zealand on 23 November after a 100-day voyage.

For Shackleton, the *Nimrod's* departure marked the end of his problems. He had opted to stay behind to raise further badly needed funds. His plan was to travel by train to the south of England, crossing the English Channel at Dover. From Calais he would take a train to Marseilles, where he would board the P&O liner *India* and journey, via the Suez Canal, to link up with the *Nimrod* in New Zealand.

In the last days left to him in England, Shackleton spent time with Emily and the children but even that brief interval was broken by an urgent message from Frank, Ernest's brother, saying he was under suspicion and facing possible arrest for the theft of the Irish 'Crown jewels'. In addition, he had debts of £1000.

What was stolen were the insignia (diamond star and badge) of the Grand Master of the Order of St Patrick (the Lord Lieutenant of Ireland) and five gold collars worn by the knights of the Order on ceremonial occasions. Otherwise, they were kept under lock and key in the tower in Dublin Castle. In the same tower Sir Arthur Vicars held his heraldic court. Among his friends and regular visitors was Frank Shackleton. Sometime between 11 June and 6 July 6 1907 the jewels were stolen and Frank Shackleton was among the chief suspects.

An inquiry was subsequently held and Frank was cleared, although rumours persisted of a whitewash, with stories that Frank was part of a homosexual ring involving members of the Dublin judiciary, which he was willing to reveal if things went against him.

While there was nothing he could do about his brother and the Crown jewels scandal, Ernest – as if there was nothing else to concern him on the eve of his departure – borrowed another £1000 from William Beardmore, to pay off Frank's debts.

Finally, on 31 October, Shackleton began his journey south. His departure from Charing Cross Station passed without attention. Emily travelled to Dover with him and the image of her as they parted was one that would haunt him on the expedition. He later wrote:

'I can see you just as you stand on the wharf and are smiling at me, my heart was too full to speak and I felt that I wanted just to come ashore and clasp you in my arms and love and care for you … If I failed to get to the pole and was within ten miles and had to turn back it would or will not mean so much sadness as was compressed in those few minutes (of parting) … I promise you that I will take every care and run no risks … I promise you darling that I will come back to you safe and well if God wishes it.'

Arriving in Australia, Shackleton discovered that over £4000 promised by his cousin, William Bell, had not materialized and that he didn't have the necessary funds to pay the crew of the *Nimrod*. He had estimated the cost of the expedition at £17,000. In the end, it would reach £50,000.

Through the generosity of the governments of New Zealand and Australia and the support of Welsh-born Edgeworth David, Professor of Geology at Sydney University, the money was raised. In return for his financial assistance, David and his colleague Douglas Mawson were to travel on the *Nimrod*.

As Shackleton travelled farther from Emily, the letters expressed his love and heartache:

'... *never again for us to be separated ... One's life is so short yet we will have good times and happy times together again ... My feelings are all too deep for words ... You stand apart entirely from the rest of the world ...You came absolutely and perfectly to my ideal of the perfect woman, I love you wildly. I have and do love you passionately.*'

On New Year's Day 1908, the *Nimrod* left Lyttelton harbour under tow from the steel steamship *Koonya*. Ten days before departure, Shackleton had realized the already overloaded *Nimrod* couldn't take enough coal on board to get her to and from Antarctica. He appealed to the New Zealand government who agreed to pay half the cost of a tow-steamer. The *Koonya* was hired and the owners, as a gesture of goodwill, opted to waive the other half of the fees.

The *Nimrod* had just 3'6" of freeboard when she left Lyttelton harbour and conditions on board were extremely cramped. For more than 1500 miles she plunged and swung on the end of a 600-foot cable, an umbilical cord to the *Koonya*.

One of the training ponies on Quail Island, outside Lyttelton, New Zealand: left to right, Tubman the horse-breaker and Dr Mackay, December 1907.

Dogs in truck at Lyttelton after Joyce had fetched them from Stewart Island, south of South Island, New Zealand, descendants of those used on the Norwegian Borchgrevink's 1898-1900 Southern Cross expedition. Joyce left, Marston the artist, Scamp (the lead dog, front centre), and Gravy.

The weather on the early stages of the journey was rough and Shackleton and his crew were reduced to signalling the steamer by flag, at one point requesting the captain of the towboat to pour oil on the sea in an attempt to calm it.

The crew suffered from seasickness and winds buffeting, the animals on board were in a worse predicament. The ponies needed constant attention and calming and at the height of the storms two had to be shot. On the other hand one of the dogs on board gave birth to six pups.

By 14 January the weather had improved and the ships encountered their first icebergs. The same day, twenty sheep carried on the *Koonya* were slaughtered and their carcasses prepared for transfer to the *Nimrod*. However, in the course of the transfer, ten of them were lost in the sea.

In the moments between supervising work, Shackleton wrote to Emily: 'I am always thinking of you and wanting you so much my heart goes out to you and the children and I am yearning to see you and have you in my arms again through long peaceful nights ... long kisses from me over the wash of uncharted seas.'

The following day, exactly two weeks after their departure, the *Nimrod* and the *Koonya* went their separate ways, the towboat heading back towards New Zealand and home, the *Nimrod* heading south into uncertain waters.

Nine days later Shackleton and his crew came in sight of the Great Ice Barrier, the Ross Ice Shelf. Shackleton's intention had been to land at King Edward Land but the large number of ice floes in the area made this scheme impossible.

'All my plans were upset by the demand of the situation,' he wrote to Emily and they were. He had no option but to land at McMurdo. Given his undertaking to Scott, he was unhappy about this but the constraints of time and pack ice which constantly thwarted any progress left him with no alternative.

Eric Marshall was unhappy with Shackleton's decision. He saw it as a direct betrayal of Scott.

'He [Shackleton] hasn't got the guts of a louse,' he wrote, 'in spite of what he may say to the world on his return.' Marshall's attitude to what he saw as Shackleton's unforgivable

Nimrod, a 136-foot long barquentine built by Alexander Stephens and Sons of Dundee, Scotland, in 1865. Used as a sealer before being bought in William Beardmore's name for the 1907 expedition.

behaviour was not shared on the *Nimrod*. To most crew-members it was obvious that the pressures of time and the need to pursue their goal were of much greater importance than some egotistical demand made by Scott.

But Marshall was not convinced and, later, while at Cape Royds, wrote that Shackleton was 'vacillating, erratic and a liar, easily scared, moody and surly, a boaster'.

What Marshall didn't know was that Shackleton was not only confronting difficult decisions but he was facing serious disagreements with Rupert England, captain of the *Nimrod*. England was not a man to take risks and his natural reaction was to prevaricate. This was a luxury Shackleton could not afford. At one point, Frank Wild concluded that England had completely lost his nerve and was, in fact 'off his rocker'.

Eventually Edgeworth David intervened and restored peace and Shackleton realized the captain's word could and did overrule that of the expedition leader. Later, England was to be replaced as captain of the *Nimrod* by F. P. Evans, former captain of the *Koonya*.

The clashes between Marshall and Shackleton on the one hand, and England and Shackleton on the other, showed the difficulties involved in maintaining calm on a long expedition where a crew lived in such close proximity.

Not everything, however, was negative. Other events drew people together. One such occurred on 31 January.

In an awful accident, Second Officer Aeneas Mackintosh was hooked in the eye as the crew of the *Nimrod* began moving cargo in preparation for unloading. Later that day Marshall operated, having knocked Macintosh out with chloroform. Using the only pair of curved scissors on board and improvising with retractor hooks made from rigging wire, he excised the eye.

On 3 February Cape Royds on Ross Island was chosen as the spot for base camp and the motor-car was landed under the supervision of driver and mechanic Bernard Day. Marshall filmed the event.

15 February was Shackleton's birthday, and Marshall gave him a letter which Emily had entrusted to him before he sailed from England. It read:

'*This letter is for your birthday 15th February to tell you I am thinking of you all day long as I always shall be while you are away ... They* [the children] *will always kiss your*

*Aeneas Mackintosh
(1879-1916), shortly
after losing his eye
in an accident
unloading cargo on
31 January 1908.*

*Interior of
Shackleton's hut, 1971.
(Courtesy David Elliot)*

*photograph night and morning and Ray will pray
"God bless my daddy and bring him safe home to us."
… Oh darling it is hard to write cheerfully … I shall
be wondering if you found a good landing place.'*

A week later, on 22 February, the *Nimrod* depart-
ed for New Zealand and Shackleton and his expeditionary force began their work in earnest. Again,
he wrote to Emily about the weather and his troubles with England, concluding: 'I am longing for the time when I can clasp you again to my arms darling and hold our children in my
arms again, that will be next year please God.'

Shackleton was back in the Antarctic, back where he had dreamed of being, back where the nightmare of illness had previously robbed him of the chance to prove himself. All the obstacles of finance and organization and doubt were behind him. Now the mission was clear. Ahead lay the object of his ambition – the South Pole.

Eleven days after the ship's departure a party of six – David, Mackay, Mawson, Adams, Marshall and Brocklehurst – set off for Mount Erebus, an active volcano some 13,370 foot high. The party made it to the summit on 10 March, but Brocklehurst suffered badly frost-bitten feet. He celebrated his twenty-first birthday in a blizzard almost 9000 feet up the mountain, eating ship's biscuits and chocolate. As a result of the frostbite he would have one of his toes amputated a month later by Marshall. Apart from this mishap, the expedition was a success.

The party returned to camp on 11 March bringing information on the height of the mountain, the position and state of craters and its geological significance. More importantly, from Shackleton's point of view, the expedition proved the stamina of the men and their ability to work well together.

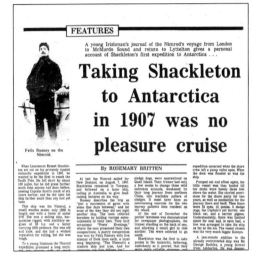

Felix Rooney (1885-1965) was a young Irishman on the Nimrod. In his diary he described the journey as, 'so rough the ship would roll the milk out of your tea'.

When Shackleton had travelled on the *Discovery* he had taken a typewriter to produce the *South Polar Times*, a monthly expedition magazine.

This time, however, he was prepared for the production of a far more ambitious publication. *Aurora Australis* was to be the first book written, edited (by Shackleton), illustrated, printed and bound in the Antarctic. With this in mind, he'd sent Joyce and Wild on a three-week crash course in printing and typesetting with Sir Joseph Causton, who loaned a printing and etching press to the expedition, as well as supplying paper and ink. All of this equipment was kept in the hut at Cape Royds in Joyce and Wild's chaotic cubicle, known as 'The Rogues' Retreat'. With the press in place and the typecase laid out, there wasn't room to lift, much less to swing, a penguin.

Aurora Australis. First book printed and bound in Antarctica; the sheep-backed Venesta (packing-case) boards were bound by the mechanic Bernard Day. Apparently 100 copies were produced in the Hut at Cape Royds but only about 65 have been account-ed for to date. This copy was presented by Shackleton to his daughter Cecily. Kidney soup stencil indicated the original contents of the case. They brought 2500 cases with stores on the trip. (Christies catalogue)

Not alone was space limited but the conditions in which they worked on the project were less than ideal. Often the ink had to be kept liquid by placing a candle under the ink-plate. Despite difficulty, confusion and clutter the pair produced, at the rate of two pages per day, *Aurora Australis*, with its proud declaration: 'Published at the winter quarters of the British Antarctic expedition, 1907, during the winter months of April, May, June, July, 1908. Illustrated with lithographs and etchings; by George Marston. Printed at the sign of 'The Penguins' by Joyce and Wild. Latitude 77 degrees 32' South Longitude 166 degrees 12' East Antarctica. (All rights reserved).'

The finished product was bound with boards from packing cases, backed with sheep-skin and sewn with green silk cord by the motor engineer Bernard Day. Individual copies were identified by the names on the particular packing cases. One volume might be the Irish Stew copy, another the Kidney Soup copy, and so on.

During those bitter winter months, three of the seven ponies died or had to be shot as a result of poisoning. Two had eaten volcanic sand and the third had eaten some shavings from one of the chemical cases. The remaining four were carefully watched and schooled. Joyce, meanwhile, took responsibility for training the dogs, which had become camp pets.

But there was other work to be done, too. Geological specimens were collected. Meteorological records were kept. The car was tested. In the darkness of the long nights the men took it in turns to cook and there was widespread use of the expedition library. The gramophone was played constantly and Marston was involved in organizing theatrical productions.

There were occasional outbursts, particularly from Shackleton, but they tended to end as quickly as they had begun and were more than compensated for by his genuine concern for each of the men who accompanied him.

The deaths of the three ponies were to be of greater consequence than might have first been imagined. Shackleton's intention had been to have a party of six on the Polar expedition. But with only four ponies surviving, he revised the figure down by two. As July wore on and the departure date approached, he chose the members of the party.

Shackleton recognized the scientific significance of the journey to the South Magnetic Pole. David and Mawson were the obvious choices for that and Mackay was chosen as the medical man on the trip.

Otherwise, there were specific people suited to specific tasks. Day was the mechanic and would be needed to drive the car when it was possible to use it. Priestley was to undertake long-term geological research in the western mountains. Murray was to be in command at the base camp. That left seven men in the running for the Polar attempt – Adams, Marshall, Brocklehurst, Joyce, Wild, Marston and Shackleton.

Following medical examinations, Marshall concluded that Brocklehurst, still recovering from the loss of his toe, and Joyce, who had a weak pulse and liver problems, were unfit for the full trip. He also noted that Shackleton had a murmur in his heart and watched him closely throughout the expedition.

While there were problems to be faced in Antarctica, other problems had been left by Shackleton for his brother-in-law, Herbert Dorman, to solve. On 12 June Herbert wrote to

Emily, bemoaning the fact that money was hard to come by: 'I heard from WB [William Beardmore] this morning. He does not see his way to assist further, and seems vexed with E(rnest) because he lent him £1000 shortly before he left which was to have been repaid in 3 weeks. It was not repaid and E never even wrote from New Zealand ... It is a great anxiety to me to feel that I am landed with the responsibility of finding the money for fitting out the *Nimrod* and bringing back the expedition. I want something like £7000 and heaven only knows where it is to come from.'

Herbert, more than anyone, was aware of the financial mess Shackleton left in his wake, and of the dire financial straits in which his sister found herself. In mid-July he wrote to her again: 'If you want £50 or £100 meantime you have only to let me know ... I think you had better *not* write to Mrs Beardmore at present.'

Later, he wrote cheering Emily up: 'Fortunately we Dormans stick together and we shall do the trick somehow. I am getting used to these financial anxieties about the expedition and happily each new worry wears off in a few hours.'

On 22 September, having spent the winter months preparing equipment and clothing, Adams, Marshall, Marston, Wild, Day and Shackleton set off with the motor car and sledges to lay Depot A, 120 miles south of the base. The car proved useful on part of the journey but the brunt of the hauling was borne by the men themselves.

Eleven days later, on 3 October, David, Mawson and Mackay set off to locate the South Magnetic Pole. Their expedition would last 122 days and set a sledging record distance of 1260 miles.

On 29 October the reduced party of four – Adams, Marshall, Wild and Shackleton – set off at 10 a.m. on the 800-mile journey to the South Pole accompanied by the four ponies, each of which hauled a sledge carrying 600 pounds of provisions, enough food to last four months. A support party accompanied them with another sledge as far as White Island.

Shackleton wrote of that morning: 'A glorious day for our start, brilliant sunshine and a cloudless sky, a fair wind from the north; in fact everything that could conduce to an auspicious beginning.'

But it was hardly to be. An hour out from base, one of the ponies went lame and the party was forced to reduce speed. Then another of the ponies kicked Adams, cutting his

knee through to the bone. At Glacier Tongue, the car stuck in the snow and had to be taken back to base. Shackleton noted: 'I pray that we may be successful for my Heart has been so much in this.'

On their second day out the men reached Hut Point and the old *Discovery* hut, which gave them a night's shelter. From there the expedition truly began. Over the following days the weather was fine and all boded well, but on 4 November the day was so dark that they were reduced to travelling by compass. Worse lay ahead. On 6 November a blizzard struck and the men were trapped in their tents for three days, cutting back on their rations and looking after the ponies, but otherwise left to their own devices. Shackleton read the comedies of Shakespeare. Marshall read the Bible.

Knowing that the men would share tents, two and two, Shackleton had decided, before they left base, that they would alternate partners on a weekly basis. He was well aware of the danger of the four splitting into two groups.

On 9 November the weather cleared and the expedition moved on uneventfully through crevasses. By 15 November they had reached Depot A. The following day, in clearer weather, they made a record journey of seventeen miles. The ponies were proving invaluable in pulling the sledges but within days, the snow crust began cutting into their fetlocks. Chinaman, the oldest of the animals, was suffering badly from fatigue and chafing and Shackleton decided he would have to be shot.

First car on Antarctica, 1 February 1908. Made at William Beardmore's Arroll-Johnston Motor Works, its 12-15 horse-power air-cooled engine was capable of up to 20 miles an hour in ideal conditions and could carry fuel for 300 miles. Bernard Day, who worked for Beardmore, was motor engineer, as he was later on Scott's Terra Nova expedition. The motor car proved to be of limited use for travelling on ice and snow, its moving parts causing a number of personal injuries.

POST CARD

½D. STAMP
HERE
FOR INLAND
USE

This Space may be used for Written or Printed
Matter.
PLASMON BISCUITS are Made Solely by
W. & R. JACOB & Co., Ltd., DUBLIN.

The Address ONLY to
be written here.

9 Regent Street
12th Nov. 1909

Dear Sir
I consider that
the use of Plasmon Biscuits
and Plasmon Chocolate greatly
helped our marching, and
that Plasmon in my opinion
is indispensable as a
food in the Polar Regions
both North and South
yours faithfully
Ernest Shackleton
Messrs Plasmon Ld
London.

*Nimrod postcard
extolling the merits of
the Plasmon Biscuits
made by W. and R.
Jacob, Dublin.*

*Below: first to the
South Magnetic Pole
16 January 1909: left
to right, Dr Mackay,
Professor David,
Douglas Mawson.*

UNION JACK HOISTED AT
SOUTH MAGNETIC POLE

Copyright

Occasional blizzards slowed progress but, even in clear weather, the men were finding the vastness of the snowfields unsettling. They were constantly edgy and nervous, feeling lost in the tremendous but pallid landscape.

On 22 November the weather cleared again. The party had made Depot B and left stores and oil for the return journey. Despite the loss of Chinaman, shot the previous night, spirits were high. But, for Adams, it must have seemed that the opening of one door by the God of the Antarctic led to the closing of another. He developed a violent toothache and it took Marshall two attempts, without proper dental equipment, to remove the tooth.

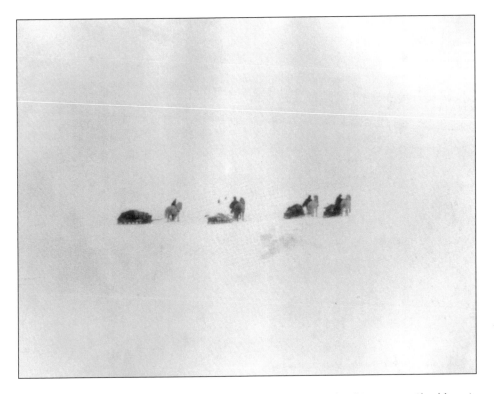

The Polar party of Adams, Marshall, Shackleton and Wild, heading into the white unknown early November 1908.

Whatever the private flights of pleasure, imagination and achievement, Shackleton's journal was as restrained as ever: 'It falls to the lot of few men to view land not previously seen by human eyes and it was with feelings of curiosity, not unmingled with awe that we watched the new mountains rise from the great unknown that lay ahead of us.'

There was still an expedition to complete and problems to surmount. Shackleton and Wild were suffering greatly from snowblindness, the drops from their painfully watering eyes freezing on their beards. What little relief there was for the snowblindness came from the use of cocaine ointment. On 26 November they celebrated reaching a new farthest point south with a bottle of orange curacao which Emily Shackleton had presented to the expedition.

The following day, a second pony, Grisi, was no longer able to go on and was shot.

There were now just two ponies and four men pulling a weight of over 1200 pounds between them. The party had travelled more than 300 miles in less than a month but the remaining pair of ponies was weakening by the day. On 1 December Quan, Shackleton's favourite, refused to pull at all and that evening he too was shot and cut up for meat. The one remaining pony, Socks, was still able to work and, while the men pulled one sledge, he followed with the other.

All along Shackleton had been attempting to avoid the mountains, but with only one pony left and time and supplies limited, he realized they would have to cross higher ground. On 3 December the men left the pony with food for the day and set out to find what Shackleton described as a 'pioneer' way south.

That day's expedition was dangerous. The men, roped together, were in crevasse country but by early afternoon they reached the summit of the hill they would name Mount Hope. From there they saw what Marshall described as 'a glacier extended as far as the eye could reach, flanked on either side by rugged ice covered mountains'. This was their way forward.

Next day, beginning the most dangerous phase of their expedition, they knew that Socks would not manage the steep and crevassed countryside.

On 6 December the party left Depot D. On the 7th Socks fell into a crevasse, almost taking Wild and a sledge with him. The pony was killed instantly, losing them a valuable food source, and Wild, hanging over the chasm by his left hand, was fortunate to survive.

As the four travelled onwards, personality clashes emerged. The extra energy being used to pull the sledges ate into the reserves of mental strength of each. Wild became convinced that Marshall was, literally, not pulling his weight and wrote in his diary: 'I sincerely wish he would fall down a crevasse about a thousand feet deep.'

Shackleton, fighting his own battles with fatigue, was charged with keeping the group together and did. His belief that 'difficulties are just things to overcome after all' wasn't just a notion. It was something he practised. He encouraged the men in any way he could. Christmas became a topic of conversation and, then, an ambition and, finally, a target in time and space. The men put aside a little food each day towards a celebration.

The four celebrated Christmas, 9500 feet up the side of the Beardmore Glacier. Shackleton produced plum pudding, brandy, cocoa, cigars and Crème de Menthe from the stores. The food may have been good but for Frank Wild the surroundings and the 48 degrees of frost were anything but salubrious. He wrote: 'May none but my worst enemies spend their Christmas in such a dreary, godforsaken place as this.'

The contrasting feelings that Christmas brought – celebration and the awareness that, one way or another, the journey was far from over – were followed in late December and the early days of January by the full realization of the task that lay ahead. Each man was now pulling a 150-lb load and the course they were taking, upward through soft snow, was backbreaking. If they were going to make the Pole they were going to be short of food, so the decision was taken to make each week's food last for ten days.

Christmas Day 9500 feet up on the Polar plateau. Wild wrote: 'May none but my worst enemies spend their Christmas in such a dreary, godforsaken place as this.' Left to right, Adams, Marshall, Wild.

The men were suffering from low temperatures. Adams was particularly badly affected by the cold and Shackleton was enduring regular migraines and giddiness. All of the men were undergoing severe tiredness and breathing problems. They found it necessary, when a halt was called, to lie in the snow for three minutes to overcome their exhaustion. Marshall, noting that their body temperatures were now two degrees below normal, advised, as a priority, that they return to the fuller rations of the previous week.

By now both Wild and Marshall privately and separately began to doubt they would get to the Pole. Shackleton, despite constant altitude sickness, wanted to continue. He was, however, fully cognizant of the responsibility he bore. There was no one else to whom he could turn. This final group of four determined men had only one leader, only one man on whom the success and safety of the team depended. On 2 January 1909 he wrote: 'I cannot think of failure yet I must look at the matter sensibly and consider the lives of those who are with me.'

Success and safety had been the watchwords, but now it was dawning on Shackleton that he might be forced to choose between the two.

On 4 January the men discussed their position and decided to leave a sixth depot, Depot F, with only a small flag to mark it. It was a risk, another blizzard might obliterate the marker and leave them with a 150-mile walk to the next depot on the way back but it was impossible to carry enough supplies to cover all eventualities and still make good time. Once the depot had been made they set off with renewed vigour. Over the following two days, in the teeth of a headwind and drifting snow, they walked twenty-five miles.

Farthest South camp after a 60-hour blizzard 133 miles from the Pole on 8 January 1909; left to right, Adams, Wild, EHS.

On the night of 6 January Shackleton wrote in his journal: 'Tomorrow we march South with the flag.' It was not to be.

The following two days saw the men confined to their tent with gales of ninety miles an hour screaming around them. Shackleton read *The Merchant of Venice*. Snow drifted into the tent. The men suffered cramp but there was no talk of going back.

On 9 January the weather cleared enough to make a 'dash' possible. The four took what supplies they could, chocolate, biscuits and sugar, and began to run 'as hard as we could' over the snow. When they couldn't run they walked. They were less than 100 miles from the Pole.

The four figures were strung out across the landscape, sometimes one ran ahead, then another. Sometimes one lagged behind, but always they moved on, relentless, their eyes, hearts and minds set on that distant, untouched spot.

Shackleton's own account of that day, written in his diary, tells the tale with all the simplicity of great achievement and courageous failure.

'The wind eased down at 1 am. At 2 am we were up had breakfast. And shortly after 4 am started south with the Union Jacks and the brass Cylinder of Stamps. At 9 am hard quick marching we were in 88.23 and there hoisted H.M's flag took possession of the Plateau in the name of H.M. and called it K.E. Plat. Rushed back over a surface hardened somewhat by the recent wind and had lunch took photo of camp Furthest south and then got away marching till 5 pm dead tired Camped lovely night – 19. Homeward Bound. Whatever regrets may be we have done our best. Beaten the South record by 366 miles the North by 77 miles. Amen.'

And that was it. The diary entry says everything and tells little. It says where they were and what they achieved. It tells nothing of the enormous pride and the enormous sadness of those four figures on the vast, wasted, snow-blown face of the Antarctic. It tells nothing of the individual feelings of sorrow and relief in those four hearts.

Forty-seven years later Adams would say that he believed another hour's march towards the Pole would have been the death of all four. But, for Shackleton, coming so far and getting so close raised the possibility of going on, one more hour, one more day. It brought, too, the temptation to decide that reaching the Pole was worth everything including life. To be the first, even if that meant death, was something that could never be taken from them. As it was, there was no guarantee of a safe return. They were 97 miles from the Pole and 730 from base. Glory beckoned across the snows, even in death it must have shone with a particular and alluring radiance.

Shackleton, however, was not to be seduced. He considered the possibility of going on himself but that would simply put pressure on the other three. Even if they did allow him to go alone, they would have been burdened by a lifelong liability of doubt.

'Whatever our regrets we have done our best,' he wrote. The decision was made and there was no time for remorse. They were, as he wrote, homeward bound, and he was as determined to get himself, and his men, safely home as he had been to get them to the Pole. That, now, became the imperative.

Shackleton was determined to get his party back safely. Wild, always loyal, wrote in his diary: 'I don't know how S. stands it; both his heels are split in four or five places, his legs are bruised and chafed, and today he has a violent headache through falls, and yet he gets along as well as anyone.'

Both Adams and Marshall advised him to ease off. Shackleton had fallen several times descending walls of ice and worried that he was holding up the others. Yet the descent over the fretted ice needed to be slow if they were to avoid serious injury or death.

The remaining sledge had been damaged and was running on one blade, and food was getting low. On 26 January 1909 the men ate the last of their biscuits and cheese. They were still twelve miles short of Depot D. Lunch that day was a cup of tea and two ounces of chocolate. Their average walking speed had reduced to one mile per hour. Three miles from the depot they were so exhausted that they had to pitch a tent and sleep. The following morning they set off at 9 a.m. but Wild and Adams both collapsed. By 1 p.m. they were still a mile from the site of the depot. They had travelled two miles in four hours. Wild and Adams could no longer continue. Marshall volunteered to go alone and bring back food.

He returned with tea, sugar, horsemeat, biscuits and pemmican: a feast. They had gone forty hours and marched sixteen miles without a proper meal.

Shackleton wrote: 'These were the worst two days ever spent in our lives.'

29 January brought another blizzard and the men were snowed into their tent. While they able to move on the following morning, they were fighting against high winds. They were also faced with the worry of finding Depot C and the extra supplies they so badly needed. In drifting snow and bad conditions, it could easily be missed.

Again, Wild was struck down, this time with dysentery, and the medicine given him by Marshall made him drowsy. Unable to eat his horsemeat, Wild's strength was going and he found it almost impossible to walk. Biscuits were the only things he could digest but these were strictly rationed. Secretly, Shackleton insisted his companion eat a biscuit saved from his own meagre supply. Wild would later write: 'I do not suppose that anyone else in the world can thoroughly realize how much generosity and sympathy was shown by this; I DO and BY GOD I shall never forget it. Thousands of pounds would not have bought me that biscuit.'

Ninety years later a single biscuit from the expedition was sold to Sir Ranulph Fiennes at a Christie's Polar auction in London for several thousand pounds.

On 4 February Shackleton scribbled in his diary: 'Cannot write any more. All down with acute dysentery. Terrible day. No march possible. Our food lies ahead and death stalks us from behind.'

The combination of physical and mental exhaustion, starvation, illness and worry were unravelling him. The *Nimrod* would return as arranged to pick them up. She would not wait indefinitely. It was extremely likely that they would miss her and be left behind.

On 7 February the weather improved and the men began to track the snow mounds they had left on their outward journey. Their rate of walking increased but not dramatically. They were still exhausted and hungry and food was a constant subject of conversation. On 10 February they reached Depot B and feasted on the liver of Chinaman. Five days later, during the 85-mile trek to Depot A, Shackleton celebrated his thirty-fifth birthday. His three colleagues presented him with a cigarette made from shreds of loose tobacco they'd saved.

Amazingly, in the midst of all this uncertainty and misery, Shackleton asked Wild to accompany him on another trip south: even more amazingly, Wild agreed.

Shackleton also suggested that, should the *Nimrod* be gone, they consider the possibility of using a rowing boat to get back to New Zealand. Little did he know that an epic journey in a rowing boat would loom large in his future.

On 20 February the men sighted Depot A at midday and reached it at four that afternoon. The first thing they did was to

Chinaman, one of Shackleton's favourites, was nearly lost slipping in to the water on arrival in Antarctica. The oldest of the four ponies on the Polar journey, and the first to be shot on 21 November to provide meat for Depot B.

dig out the buried stores and cook themselves a decent meal. Marshall made 'the best pudding I ever tasted' – a mixture of broken biscuits and blackcurrant jam.

Three days later they reached a depot left by Joyce – accidentally seeing the flag that marked it well off their course – and had a supper of sausages and a breakfast the following morning of porridge and eggs. The dramatic change of diet brought on another severe attack of dysentery in Marshall, leaving him too ill to travel. Shackleton and Wild went forward to Hut Point to get help. The journey involved a detour of seven miles because of worsening weather and Shackleton suffered constant headaches. What awaited him was the last thing he needed.

A note had been left, telling the men the *Nimrod* would wait for them, at Glacier Tongue, until 26 February. It was now 28 February. What Shackleton couldn't know was whether the captain of the *Nimrod* was going to wait for another couple of days at Cape Royds or sail for New Zealand on the 26th. It was quite possible that they had been left behind to winter on the ice.

Wild and Shackleton spent the night in the *Discovery* hut and the following morning started signalling for the *Nimrod*. They set an outhouse on fire and, later, lit a carbide flare using their own urine, as there was no other liquid available.

On the *Nimrod*, Maxwell, peering through the blizzard a quarter of a mile off shore, saw the flare. The ship headed back immediately. By one in the morning Wild and Shackleton were clambering aboard to be greeted by the question everyone wanted to ask: 'Did you reach the Pole?'

They hadn't, but amazingly they'd all survived.

Having eaten and rested for a couple of hours, Shackleton led a party back to pick up Marshall and Adams. By 4 March all four men were safely aboard ship, though Marshall, absurdly wearing new finneskoes (reindeer-fur boots), slipped on ice and was almost killed.

By his own calculations, Shackleton's party had walked, including relay work, 1725 miles and 300 yards in 126 days. They had gone 366 miles farther south than anyone had previously done. And they had all returned safely.

Failure was hardly the word to describe what had been achieved and withstood.

What awaited them in England was a divided response. Shackleton and his team would be

The southern party rejoined the Nimrod *on 3 March 1909; left to right, Wild, Shackleton, Marshall and Adams.*

greeted as heroes by the populace but for individuals like Edward Wilson, his one-time friend, the news that Shackleton had 'trespassed' on Scott's territory meant only one thing: betrayal.

He wrote: 'As for Shackleton, I feel the less said the better – I am afraid he has become a regular wrong 'un, and I know too much of all that has gone on to speak about him with any pleasure at all. In fact I have broken with him completely and for good.'

Sir Clements Markham, President of the Royal Geographical Society, was another whose attitude to Shackleton hardened. At the time of the *Discovery* expedition he had written that Scott was 'fortunate in finding such an excellent and zealous officer as Ernest Shackleton'. After his return from the *Nimrod* expedition he altered his notes: 'He seemed a steady young man.'

Shackleton might have risked life and limb, he might have taken his men beyond the point where they could count on deliverance, and significantly beyond previous expeditions, but he had fallen foul of those whose main concern was that he had trodden, almost literally, on Scott's snowshoes. Never mind that Scott, in turn, would use Shackleton's route up the Beardmore Glacier and follow his example by using ponies. He might be the darling of the man and woman in the street; he might even be their hero; but according to Scott he was 'A professed liar and a plausible rogue.'

The geographic establishment would never forgive the upstart Irishman who hadn't played by their rules.

7

Knighthood and the Public Man

1909–1914

When word reached Emily Shackleton that her husband had made the farthest journey south she told the *Daily Mirror* on 27 March 1909 that Ernest was 'a born organizer as all the world can see, and the love and admiration of his comrades prove his worth as a man'. The five years that followed that achievement, however, were, in differing ways, to be every bit as testing for the couple. Eleven weeks after she gave the interview, on 12 June, Shackleton arrived in England to a very public hero's welcome.

He had left New Zealand on 15 April, having earlier lectured in Wellington Town Hall, raising £300 that he immediately donated to local charities. After a formal farewell lunch given by the Prime Minister, Sir Joseph Ward, and his ministers, Shackleton gave a gracious, entertaining speech and extolled those New Zealanders who'd assisted him financially and through their goodwill and encouragement. He also noted, as he was to do time and again, that this had been a group effort of which he was only one member.

The following day he sailed on the *Riverina* with a Maori cry of farewell ringing in his ears. He left with unbridled elation, allowing him to write to Emily that he was coming home for good. 'I … want … to tell you how much I love you how much I have missed you all this time and how I long to see you and our little ones again. Never again my beloved will there be such a separation as this has been.'

The success of his New Zealand lecture, the promises made and the opportunities in the offing – the expectation of earning up to £10,000 from lecturing and £20,000 from the sale of commemorative stamps, plus the proceeds from the book he planned – were responsible for this surge of optimism. He was falling into the trap of believing most of what he was told and everything that he imagined. The faraway hills of England were green, just as the wildernesses of Antarctica would be when remembered from England.

In Australia, a series of successful lectures reinforced his sense that financial security lay at last in his own hands. Leaving on the *India*, he set about writing his book with the help of Edward Saunders.

Saunders had first seen Shackleton in 1901 when, as a young reporter of nineteen, he visited the *Discovery* in Lyttelton. Six years later, he interviewed Shackleton before the *Nimrod* left New Zealand. Now, two years on, Shackleton was back in Lyttelton and employing him as his confidential secretary for four months from 15 April, on a salary of £10 per week plus expenses and a return ticket to New Zealand. Beyond their working relationship, the two men became firm friends and they began the book which Saunders would shape from Shackleton's memories.

The journey from Australia to Port Said wasn't all work, and other passengers and crew-members regularly had to compete with raucous laughter in the dining-room. Shackleton, Armytage, Adams and Mackintosh made a drama of mealtimes with what one passenger described as Shackleton's 'Irish wit and inexhaustible supply of funny stories'.

Transferring to the mail boat *Isis* at Port Said in Egypt, Shackleton arrived in Dover on 12 June. The plan was for a quiet family reunion but what awaited was the first of many public receptions, this one led by the Mayor of Dover. Like it or not, Shackleton was now public property. His life was not to be his own for a very long time.

On 14 June he travelled by train to London. The reception was beyond even his vivid imagination. The station was packed and outside the scenes were chaotic. The top brass of the geographical world were there to meet their returning hero. Among the platform party were Scott, come to meet and laud the 'professed liar', and Markham, who suggested to Scott that Shackleton was suffering from 'a swollen head'.

Shackleton, as always, made a speech not about himself but about his men. The word *I* rarely featured in his lectures or speeches. Heroic he might seem to others, but he knew he was one of a tightly knit team and without it there could be no survival. It was a lesson Scott might have learned.

The official speeches over, Shackleton moved outside to meet the throng who had come to see this ordinary man who had done an extraordinary thing. In the public mind, heroic and human, he had organized his own expedition, come within miles of the South Pole and, in so doing, reached the farthest south by the greatest distance. He was a man they admired, loved, wanted to see and hear and touch. His arrival in London had echoes of Christ's entry into Jerusalem. It was reported that people took the horses out of the shafts of the coach in which their hero was travelling and pulled it by hand. Whether this is truth or rumour matters little. Shackleton was the people's hero. Nor did it occur to those who came to see him that knives were being unsheathed in the Royal Geographical Society or that Sir Clements Markham, who spoke with apparent sincerity of his long friendship with Shackleton, was already his chief critic. All the people saw was their champion, all they heard were his easy words and unceremonious introductions to his travelling companions.

While cliques within the RGS set about undermining him, praise poured in from fellow travellers, the Norwegians Nansen and Amunsden.

Nansen referred admiringly to Shackleton's 'remarkable deed, and important discoveries and the excellent way in which he led his men through all dangers'. Amunsden wrote: 'The English nation has by the deed of Shackleton won a victory which can never be surpassed.'

While the public clamour pleased Shackleton, praise of his peers was every bit as important. He was receiving recognition, from his equals, for the scientific work he had done in the Antarctic.

In one of the few quiet moments available to them, Shackleton and Emily discussed the expedition's failure. He asked her whether 'a live donkey is better than a dead lion?' and she replied: 'Yes, darling, as far as I'm concerned.' In her own words, she said: 'We left it at that.'

Much of the praise showered on Shackleton benefited the RGS by association. Markham strongly believed that Scott was England's man for the South Pole and that the Irishman was only queering the pitch for his candidate. He put Shackleton's efforts alongside those of the other 'foreigners' who were simply a nuisance, though he was not willing to say as much publicly. He knew that this was not the time to attempt to remove the halo.

J. Scott Keltie, Secretary of the RGS was to some extent Markham's stalking-horse. He was responsible for confirming Shackleton's claims about how far south he had travelled. He wrote to Shackleton: '[the] difficulty of taking any observations under the conditions must have been fearfully trying, but still, I have no doubt you established your latitude to your complete satisfaction.'

Meanwhile, Markham was writing to Major Leonard Darwin, President of the RGS, damaging Shackleton and laying claims not just for Scott but for himself: 'As I am responsible for having started all this Antarctic business, I think it right that I should send you a note ... Shackleton's failure to reach the South Pole when it could have been done by another, and is really a matter of calculation, rather aggravates me ... I cannot accept the latitudes ... I do not believe it.'

The man challenging Shackleton's claims and calling him a liar had sat safely in London, apart from holidaying in Portugal, through the whole affair.

Shackleton found himself replying in the *Geographical Journal*, to slurs as much as to direct accusations:

'*The latitude observations ... were taken with the theodolite ... Variation was ascertained by means of a compass attached to the theodolite, and the steering compasses were checked accordingly ... The last latitude observation on the outward journey was taken in 87 degrees 22' S. and the remainder of the distance towards the south was calculated by sledge meter and dead reckoning.*'

One wonders whether Scott would have faced the same innuendo.

Shackleton's Irishness, however, was viewed differently by Sir Arthur Conan Doyle who, according to *The Yorkshire Reporter*, referred to Shackleton as a 'fellow-Irishman' and urged people to 'think of what Ireland has done for the Empire ... think of that flag flapping down yonder on the snow field, planted there by an Irishman'.

In Dublin, at a time of resurgent national feeling, *The Weekly Freeman* writer was unequivocal: 'Let there be no mistake, the Shackletons are Irish,' he wrote. *The Dublin Express* referred to 'the qualities that were his heritage as an Irishman, the dash and buoyant enthusiasm, the cheerful unshakeable courage'.

At a ceremony in London's Albert Hall on 28 June, the Prince of Wales, representing the king who was unable to attend, gave Shackleton a gold medal 'in recognition of his great and unique achievement'.

The presentation itself had been the centre of continuing controversy. A letter on 19 April from the RGS to Cuthbert Bayes, who would strike the medal, had informed him that the Society did 'not propose to make the Medal so large as that which was awarded to Capt. Scott'. Three weeks later Bayes received another letter telling him that the Society were, in fact, going 'to let Mr Shackleton have a Medal of the same size'.

For this he and his comrades had tramped the wastes of Antarctica.

Shackleton in 1909, looking uncharactistically 'civilized'.

On the night of the presentation, Scott proposed the vote of honour to Shackleton and thanked him for the 'very substantial addition he had made to human knowledge, but most of all because he has shown us a glorious example of British pluck and courage'.

They made a striking pair on a public platform and while Scott's tribute was well received, neither man liked or trusted the other. For Scott, Shackleton was a threat, a man who had outdone him but had also failed to reach the Pole. Scott had access to money and support and, barring a disaster, would be back in the Antarctic before his rival.

The weeks that followed Shackleton's homecoming might have been intended as a quiet time in which to get to know his children but, instead, they became an endless social round. Lectures, dinners, meetings, a visit to his old school, a talk at the Authors' Club, the presentation of the freedom of the borough of Lewisham, were all part of what was expected of this very public man. The whirl culminated in a visit to Buckingham Palace where the king invested him as a Commander of the Royal Victorian Order. But the adventure was now over and had to be paid for.

Shackleton's book was due out in November and he was hopeful it would sell well. Between debts and money due for guarantees, the expedition was £20,000 short of funds. It had cost almost £45,000. Some of those who had acted as guarantors might not seek repayment but there still remained a small fortune to be found.

Herbert Dorman, Emily's brother, had done most of the financial drudgery for the expedition. While Shackleton was in the public eye, Herbert Dorman was in the firing line. Demands for money for the upkeep of the *Nimrod*, for men's wages – still, in many cases, unpaid – and for outstanding bills for equipment and provisions meant that the project was in severe financial trouble. Dorman even considered launching a public appeal through the *Daily Mail*. The Dorman family, particularly Daisy, gave unstintingly to help offset their brother-in-law's indebtedness.

To many of his crew, however, the public man being fêted in London was the same individual who owed them wages. They needed the money, and they too had families to support. Shackleton's habit of taking a taxi and keeping it on call for a day at a time, often with the meter literally running outside people's houses, did little to maintain his former crewmen's esteem for him.

Again, this is the paradox of Shackleton. He never had any intention of abandoning his men and the social round on which he found himself was necessary to build public support. At the same time he had the unhappy knack of forgetting that other people had troubles, too, and that good intentions make poor meals.

By August he found himself releasing a statement to the newspapers explaining his financial problems. On 19 August the Prime Minister, Asquith, wrote to Shackleton telling him that the government 'have decided to recommend Parliament to make a grant of £20,000 to meet portion of the expenditure'.

Immediately, Shackleton was out of the darkness and back in the sunlight of his own ambition. 'Isn't it splendid,' he wrote to Emily, '£20,000 will be paid in, in a few days … Just think of your Boy getting £20,000 from the country: What Oh!!'

On 27 August the *Nimrod* arrived in England and the following day she docked at London's Temple Pier and was opened to the public. Over the next eight weeks more than 30,000 people visited the ship and over £2000 was raised for charity. From late October, she toured various British ports raising funds for good causes.

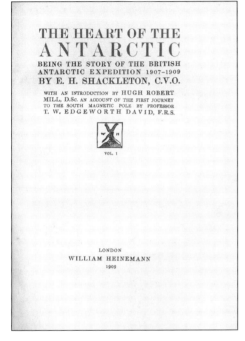

THE HEART OF THE
ANTARCTIC
BEING THE STORY OF THE BRITISH
ANTARCTIC EXPEDITION 1907-1909
BY E. H. SHACKLETON, C.V.O.

WITH AN INTRODUCTION BY HUGH ROBERT
MILL, D.Sc. AN ACCOUNT OF THE FIRST JOURNEY
TO THE SOUTH MAGNETIC POLE BY PROFESSOR
T. W. EDGEWORTH DAVID, F.R.S.

VOL. 1

LONDON
WILLIAM HEINEMANN
1909

Title-page of The Heart of the Antarctic, *Shackleton's account of the* Nimrod *expedition. Shackleton dictated much of the book to Edward Saunders, a New Zealand reporter with the* Lyttelton Times *who travelled back with him to England during the summer of 1909. They worked well together; Saunders refused acknowledgment.*

In the last week of September Shackleton gave a lecture at Balmoral for the king. He was to be back in royal company eight weeks later but, in the meantime, he lectured in Copenhagen, Stockholm and Gothenburg before travelling to Brussels where his lecture was translated by De Gerlache.

The Heart of the Antarctic was published at the beginning of November, translated simultaneously in seven languages and in an American edition. It was well received, being both a good story well told and a scientific account accessible to the lay person. The one dissenting voice was that of J. Scott Keltie, who wrote: 'We may … cherish a hope that the Union Jack will be carried across the hundred miles or so which have been left untrodden by Shackleton … This we may be assured will be accomplished by Captain Scott in the next year or two.'

To crown the success of the book, Shackleton's name appeared in the king's birthday honours list – Ernest Shackleton, merchant seaman, was to become Sir Ernest. This honour, however, wouldn't pay the bills and he set off on a gruelling lecture tour that took him to all major British cities and to Paris over the following eight weeks. In the midst of this hectic schedule, on 14 December 1909, he received the first Antarctic knighthood to be bestowed since that of Sir James Ross in 1843.

Not that the knighthood made any difference, he was still Shackleton, man of the people and the people flocked to see him. The electricity of the Antarctic adventure was boosted by the charge of public acclaim. His lectures were never less than entertaining, whether relating the antics of penguins or the experiences of his comrades. His way with words and willingness to open himself to his listeners warmed his audiences.

After Christmas at home in Edinburgh, the early weeks of 1910 saw Emily and himself off again. They travelled to Rome and then Berlin and Vienna. In Germany and Austria he lectured in German, having learned his lecture off by heart. By the time he had reached Vienna, he felt comfortable enough with the language to answer questions in German.

The story is told that someone said of him that, if asked, he'd lecture in Chinese. To which he replied: 'But I *do* know some Chinese, I *could* lecture in it!'

Shackleton and Emily parted ways in Germany, she returning to the children, he going on to Budapest and St Petersburg. Wherever he went, rumours followed. He was going south again. He was joining a German expedition. He had every right to go at the same time as Scott. Some of these rumours must have reached Emily because he wrote to her, reassuring her that 'the main thing … is to see that we are all right financially before starting again'.

Back in Britain in February, the lecture tour continued and in mid-March he travelled, with Emily, on the *Lusitania* to New York. He left behind him a discussion on the relevance of the race for the South Pole. Geographers were adamant that research rather than competition was important. The South Pole of itself was of no value. Exploration and, as *The Times* put it, 'knowledge of the world's geography' were the important issues.

Arriving in New York in the last week of March he was entertained, in turn, by the British ambassador, the American President Taft and the American Geographical Society who awarded him their Gold Medal.

America, meanwhile, was taking to the Irishness in Shackleton. What they expected was a stuffy lecturer. What they got was a spontaneous, witty, engaging and dramatic talker who held them spellbound. Even the accent – once a problem for Shackleton – was received as a breath of fresh air. It was softer, less formal, than the British accents of the embassy staff. Knight and unionist he might be, but democratic America was impressed.

Not satisfied with lecturing, Shackleton had hoped to fit in a visit trip north to investigate the Alaskan landscape between the Mackenzie River and Point Barrow, but the trip fell through.

There were a few moments of unease. Shackleton's agent was charging people to attend his lectures while the American Geographical Society had a tradition of free admission. A compromise was reached and he lectured, for free, to the inner circle of the society, before going about the business of earning his living from the paying public. In May the news came

that the king had died. Shackleton, who'd had a good relationship with the monarch, was deeply upset.

The *New York Sun* correspondent, meanwhile, was impressed by the 'perils he and his party went through [which] were real and desperate … He never missed a chance to say what fine fellows were [those] who toiled with him.'

In Canada the reception he received was every bit as warm. Attending a war veteran's dinner he talked of 'a body of men who have been tried and who know. I thank you for allowing me to talk to you.'

Back in the United States Shackleton's tour began to run out of steam. Poor advertising meant that the crowds in New England were small and by the time he returned to Britain

Sir Edmund Walker, EHS, Professor J.J. MacKenzie, on the front steps of Long Garth, 99 St George Street, Toronto, Canada, April 1910. (Courtesy Wentworth Walker)

in mid-June his thoughts were more of the possibilities of exploring in Alaska than they were of lecturing again.

The incessant talking of the previous eight months had made some money but not a fortune. Wherever he went, reporters questioned him on the possibilities of a new expedition. They were preaching to the converted.

There were more pressing and domestic matters at hand. In July the Shackleton family left Edinburgh and moved to Sheringham in Norfolk. That same month he went to see Scott off at Waterloo Station. While Scott was polite, his wife, Kathleen, was cold towards Shackleton.

A month later he was back on the lecture circuit, moving up the east coat of England into Scotland and back into northern England, to the news that Amunsden, on board the *Fram,* was also going south with the intention of reaching the Pole. With this in mind Shackleton headed for Germany in November.

On one of these trips he wrote to Emily telling her he was 'never again going south'.

If he meant what he said, it was undoubtedly brought on by the frustration of the lecture circuit. The depots were replaced by hotel rooms, the wilderness by a sea of faces on another unending journey in search of financial security.

The Germany Shackleton reached in November 1910 was not the same country he had visited earlier that year. The shadow of imminent war was stretching across Europe. From Cologne, he wrote to Emily: 'I can see a strong anti-English feeling in Germany … when the picture of the Queen's flag is shown there is stony silence … If things do not go better soon I will think very seriously of chucking the whole thing.'

From Germany Shackleton travelled to Poland and Switzerland. Apart from his lecturing he was still trying make money and the opportunity to invest in mining in Hungary was the latest solution to his ever-present problem. He was also promoting his Tabard cigarettes and an investment he had made in a taxi company in England was giving him a reasonable return, but none of these enterprises was going to keep Emily and himself and their children in any kind of comfort. This, however, didn't stem another of his rushes of optimism. A letter to Emily from Stuttgart, on a day when he had received an order for 20,000 Tabard cigarettes, was full of good tidings: '… that means £17 profit. If I can devote more time I will get much more like this.' On 14 December he was in Dublin, lecturing in Earlsfort Terrace less than

Lady DUDLEY'S SCHEME

FOR THE

**Establishment of District Nurses
in the Poorest Parts of Ireland.**

ON BEHALF OF THE ABOVE,

Sir Ernest Shackleton

Will give his Illustrated Lecture on

'Nearest the South Pole'

In the

**UNIVERSITY BUILDINGS,
EARLSFORT TERRACE,**

TUESDAY, Dec. 14th, at 8.0.

The Chair will be taken by

His Excellency The LORD LIEUTENANT.

SEATS, £1 1s. 10/6 7/6 5/- UNRESERVED, 2/6
Doors open at 7.15. Carriages at 10.
Plan and Tickets at Offices L.D.N.S., 30, Molesworth
Street; and Messrs. Cramer, Wood & Co.

The Lecture will be fully illustrated by

Kinematograph Pictures

And Photographs taken during the Expedition.

Shackleton gave a lecture at Earlsfort Terrace, Dublin in 1910.

two miles from the house in Donnybrook where he had spent the last years of his Irish childhood. Before the lecture, he was guest of honour at a dinner in the Gresham Hotel in Sackville Street. The people of Dublin, as elsewhere in the country, greeted and fêted him as an Irishman and he responded by telling them that he had been born Irish and he was still Irish.

The trip to Ireland, which also took in Belfast and Cork, brought to an end a year in which he had given 123 lectures, 50 of those in November and December alone. It was a year in which he had travelled over 20,000 miles and addressed more than a 250,000 people.

Making money was a difficulty for Shackleton, but staying at home, making ends meet, never being sure of where the next wild idea or uncertain income lay, was every bit as difficult for Emily. When her husband was in Antarctica she had a settled if empty life. Now that he was back in Europe things were little better. To add to her depression, early in 1911 she discovered she was pregnant again.

When he was in England, business seemed to take Shackleton more and more to London, leaving Emily with the children in Norfolk. This isolation and her pregnancy were a recipe for deep unhappiness. She and her husband had come from warm, happy families and he, when about, was generally an entertaining father. But his absence far outweighed his presence.

Sometimes, as on the occasion when he arrived disguised as an old man and convinced her and the children that he was his own long-lost Irish uncle, the possibilities of happiness opened before her. But there were other, longer, darker times when his life seemed much the better of the two.

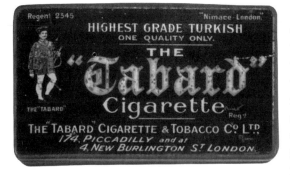

EHS formed the 'Tabard' cigarette company in 1904. The name was probably suggested by his brother Frank, the herald in Dublin Castle.

There was something of the manic-depressive in Shackleton. When life was good he was wonderful, but when boredom set in he could be unbearable. He might talk of spending more time at home but only did this when he was away, when the weight of his own guilt lay heavily on his shoulders. Back in Edinburgh or Norfolk, the trivialities of day-to-day life and the perceived demands of a wife and children were every bit as burdensome as the lack of finance. He loved his wife and children, but found living with them a challenge. He could entertain, he could swoop in and charm, but he needed to be away again, chasing money or security or achievement. She might be the base camp to which he returned, but she recognized that adventure was elsewhere.

In March 1911 Shackleton returned to Hungary, pursuing the elusive dream of a business that would bring in a lot of money. He told Emily that he wanted to 'feel I am clear of the Expedition and I have a straight road in front of me: If we live quietly for 2 or 3 years we can then do more … I want to consolidate our world.'

If those words put Emily's mind at rest, these must have raised the snowy ghosts again: 'I feel that another Expedition unless it crosses the Continent is not much.' By May, after attending at a meeting of the Aerial League of the British Empire in London, his thoughts turned to taking an aeroplane to the Antarctic.

The same month saw moves of a more practical nature, however. Emily, having enough of living in Sheringham, insisted that they move to London, where they took a house at 7 Heathview Gardens, Putney Heath. The latest move, like the initial move to Edinburgh, engaged his energy and preoccupied him for a short time. Carpets, wallpaper, even stair-rods, became the objects of his attention. For Emily, the house was something much more important, a move back to a world where she felt at home and in touch with the people she knew.

Two months later, Edward Arthur Alexander was born, on 15 July. A glorious summer of blue skies and soaring temperatures stretched ahead. But for Shackleton there was only frustration and a rising aggressiveness. Scott and Amunsden were gone south, he was stuck in London. The South Pole was, again, an object of contention but not for him.

It was also a summer when he had recurring chest pains. Nor were things at all well at home. Emily suffered from depression following Edward's birth and, more and more, Shackleton could be found visiting friends alone.

The end of the summer, and the shortening days, brought further bad news. His brother Frank, long under the shadow of suspicion for theft, was now being examined for bankruptcy. It transpired that he had debts in the region of £85,000 and had defrauded a number of people, among them Lord Ronald Sutherland-Gower and his adopted son, Frank Hird. Hird wrote to Ernest Shackleton, accusing him of being party to the fraud. Shackleton sued him for libel. Hird, however, withdrew his allegations before the case came to court.

Meanwhile Shackleton went back to things spiritual and resumed his association with Freemasonry, becoming inducted as a Second Degree Freemason in November.

The days leading up to Christmas were less than festive. A year had passed in which he had travelled and lectured, yet money was no more plentiful, business no more successful, his personal life no happier. The hankering to 'be away' was as strong as ever. There was hardship in the Antarctic, but it was a kind of hardship he could manage.

Worse was to come. On 14 December 1911, as far south as it was possible to go, his great dream came to an end.

The New Year of 1912 found Shackleton thinking actively about the possibilities of a new expedition, yet the intimations of his own eclipse were everywhere. Scott and Amundsen were moving towards the Pole, might even have reached it, for all he knew. It could only be a matter of weeks before word came of one or other having been successful.

But first there was other, more tragic news. On 15 April the *Titanic* sank in the North Atlantic with the loss of 1513 lives, having collided with an iceberg. This event, too, was to have repercussions for Shackleton.

A month later, on 17 May, the news he dreaded finally came. Amundsen had reached the South Pole. Shackleton, despite the sense of defeat, was fulsome in his praise for the new hero. He wired Amundsen, sending 'Heartiest congratulations' and wrote in the newspapers that the British people ought to acknowledge Amunsden's achievement in the same way that the Norwegian people would if Scott had reached the Pole first. He further described him as 'perhaps the greatest Polar explorer of today' and noted that (unlike Scott, who had followed his route) Amundsen 'made for himself an entirely new route'.

Kathleen Scott was not amused by Shackleton's graciousness and saw in it an attempt to denigrate her husband. She would, she said, 'willingly assist in that man's assassination,' as Roland Huntford reported in his book *Scott and Amunsden*.

Sir Clements Markham, as ever, had to have the last word and noted that Scott and his team would reach the Pole on foot, pulling their sledges, in 'the true British way'.

Amundsen, in his autobiography *My Life as an Explorer* (1928), described how after a lecture given by him in 1912 at an RGS dinner in London, its president Lord Curzon 'ended with the phrase "I therefore propose three cheers for the dogs" clearly indicating the next moment his satirical and derogatory intention by turning to me with an unnecessary calming gesture'. The insulted Amundsen called it a 'flagrant and insulting incident' and resigned his honorary fellowship of the society forthwith.

Shackleton's next engagement was the hearing into the sinking of the *Titanic*. He was called as a witness on 18 June as someone who had experience of navigation in ice. Almost immediately he and his interrogators, Sir Rufus Isaacs and Sir Robert Finlay, were at loggerheads. Suggestions were made that Shackleton's experience of ice in the northern hemisphere was limited but Shackleton stuck rigidly to his assertion that a captain on any vessel, even one travelling at six knots per hour, should be prepared to reduce speed in waters where there was a danger of icebergs. Sparks flew again when Shackleton suggested the captain of the *Titanic*, Edward John Smith, might have been under orders from the owners to maintain his speed. The sixty-two year old Smith, like Shackleton, had worked his way up through the ranks, in his case of the White Star Line, taking his first captaincy in 1887.

Ironically, when a statue of Smith was erected in Lichfield in 1914, its sculptor was Kathleen Scott.

The hearing, as so often, was a temporarily consuming issue for Shackleton. When his evidence was complete he was back to the mediocrity of real life. Even an invitation from the

Liberal Unionists to consider another attempt at a seat in Parliament held no attraction for him.

In November he was on the platform to greet Amundsen in London, one of the few senior figures in England to accord him that respect.

December saw him returning to New York, promoting his tobacco business yet still harking after a different lifestyle.

In the early months of 1913 Scott was back in the news. In February the *Terra Nova* arrived in England, bringing with it the ghosts of Scott and the men who had perished with him. The long wait was finally over. The sight of the ship docking confirmed the awful outcome of Scott's last expedition. It heralded, too, a not unsurprising upsurge in feeling for the dead explorer.

Shackleton's thoughts, however, were with the living rather than the dead, and more anxious than ever to be away from London. Frank was back in court, facing charges of fraudulently cashing a cheque.

With the Pole conquered, crossing the Antarctic continent was now the attraction. This had originally been mooted by the Scottish explorer William Bruce in 1908. His hope was that one person might put up the money for the trip in return for rights to the film footage he would take and the book and newspaper rights that could be agreed. He wrote and had printed a prospectus which summed up the objective of the expedition: 'To cross the South Polar Continent from sea to sea – from the Weddell Sea to the Ross Sea.' This was, he said, 'the last great Polar journey that can be made'.

For Emily the possibility of his being away, consumed by another great adventure, must have held some appeal for a woman who had seen her husband become morose and unsettled.

On 29 December 1913 Shackleton made his intentions public in a letter to *The Times*.

> *Sir,*
> *It has been an open secret for some time past that I have been desirous of leading another expedition to the South Polar regions.*
> *I am glad now to be able to state that, through the generosity of a friend, I can announce that an expedition will start next year with the object of crossing the South Polar continent from sea to sea.*
> *I have taken the liberty of calling the expedition 'The Imperial Trans-*

Antarctic Expedition', because I feel not only the people of these islands, but our kinsmen in all the lands under the Union Jack will be willing to assist towards the carrying out of the full programme of exploration to which my comrades and myself are pledged.

The announcement brought immediate protests from the Austrian, Felix König, who was planning an expedition into Antarctica from the Weddell Sea. Shackleton dismissed his protests, claiming the transcontinental crossing was much more important. Relations between Britain and the Germanic peoples were deteriorating at a rapid rate and Shackleton's stand was lauded as a patriotic one.

Interestingly, despite the wave of patriotism sweeping Britain, the Royal Geographical Society came down on König's side, although Shackleton was voted a grant of £1000 by the Society. More surprisingly, his long-time admirer, H.R. Mill, refused to support the idea on the basis that it was too dangerous.

The most venemous opposition came from Sir Clements Markham, who wrote to J. Scott Keltie, secretary of the RGS, on 14 January: 'I have been astounded at the absurdity of Shackleton's plan, alike useless and expensive and designed solely for self-advertisement.' In a 14-page report to the RGS Council three days later he questioned his qualifications: 'Shackleton's great grandfather had a pupil another great man, Edmund Burke, who habitually tinged facts with the colours of his own wishes or imagination. This may be a desireable habit for an orator or a journalist but not for an explorer.'

Shackleton was determined. He argued that much scientific research could be done on the journey and he gave details of his plans. There were to be two ships. He would take 120 trained dogs. The main mode of transporting supplies would be two large sledges with aeroplane engines and propellers.

In February he met with the RGS and told them that 'no expedition should set forth without the one object of being purely scientific ... My desire is to cross the Antarctic continent ... the members of it [the expedition] are the agents of the British nation. If I said differently I would be untrue to my conviction.'

In spite of scientific and patriotic cards, there were many sceptical voices in the RGS. Asked about the use of radios on the expedition, for example, Shackleton accepted that radios would be helpful: 'if I had the money,' he added, he would not 'want to communicate with England at all'.

This was his expedition and, while he might ask for support, he was not about to alter his plans for anyone. The very spirit which made him a hero of the people was the trait that annoyed the RGS members.

While few were willing to put money into the expedition, five thousand applied to join the enterprise. Among the applications was one from 'three sporty girls … [who are] willing to undergo any hardships … If our feminine garb is inconvenient, we should just love to don masculine attire … we do not see why men should have all the glory.' Tempted or not, Shackleton politely declined their offer.

In October another fraud case involving Frank came to a head at the Old Bailey and he was sentenced to fifteen months hard labour for defrauding Mary Browne, an elderly lady, of £1000. More than ever, Shackleton wished to be away from the trouble his brother hauled in his wake. The publication of Scott's diaries the following month brought further pressures. References to Shackleton were mischievous, blaming him for miscalculations that had, supposedly, thrown Scott's progress into turmoil. The public were unaware that the diaries had been altered by Kathleen Scott, Sir Clements Markham and their publisher Reginald Smith before publication, to copper-fasten Scott's courageous image in the public eye.

One of the people who refused to accept the story as told in the diary was Caroline Oates, mother of Captain Oates who had died on the Scott expedition. Using her son's letters as a reference point, she was convinced that Scott's version did not tally with the version her son suggested. Little by little, through interviews with the survivors of the expedition, she elicited a story that convinced her that her son and the others who died had been needlessly sacrificed.

Not alone did she question the legend being built around Scott, but she was driven towards Shackleton and the things he stood for and, in time, she became friendly with Emily.

December brought a change of fortune for Shackleton with the government agreeing to give £10,000 towards his expedition; the rest he would have to find himself. Despite appeals to friends and business people, money was slow in coming. Shackleton, however, went ahead and bought a 350-ton wooden Norwegian ship, the *Polaris*, for £14,000.

The *Polaris* had been built in 1913 specifically to work in the ice but her prospective

The Shackleton family at Eddie's christening, Eastbourne, 19 September 1911.

Standing, left to right: Emily, Daisy Dorman (Emily's sister), Rev. Frank Ayers, EHS, Frank Dorman. Seated, left to right: Ethel Ayers (EHS's sister) with her daughter Joyce, nurse holding Eddie, Elizabeth Dawson-Lambton, Raymond and, front left, Cecily.

owners, Lars Christensen and Adrien de Gerlache, had been unable to find the money to pay for her and she was put up for sale. She sat, unwanted for over a year before Shackleton bought her and immediately renamed her the *Endurance*, after the family motto.

Finding large donations hard to come by, Shackleton changed his approach and asked several hundred wealthy people to contribute £50 each. Lord Rosebery sent a note with his £50, telling Shackleton that 'by the time you return ... you will not find anyone in England with £50 left'. Markham, as usual, was quick to denigrate Shackleton's idea, describing him as 'worn out'.

Two people of very differing backgrounds suddenly came to Shackleton's rescue. Sir James Caird, the jute magnate who lived in Dundee, agreed to give £24,000, and Janet Stancomb-Wills also offered Shackleton substantial financial support.

Janet Stancomb-Wills had been adopted as a child by Sir W.H. Wills, the tobacco tycoon. She was a town councillor in Ramsgate and unmarried. While her initial interest in Shackleton was altruistic, in time she became a close friend and confidante. She was also to act as a benefactor to the Shackleton family, helping out with the children's school fees and acting as a sympathetic listener to Emily's woes.

Even though finances weren't fully in place, Caird and Stancomb-Wills' monies ensured that there was enough to make the expedition possible. In a moment of depression, he had said, 'I suppose I am really no good for anything but the Antarctic.' What he was good at was again within his sights. He was back in the business he loved more than anything: going south, adventuring.

8

The Endurance and Aurora

1914–1917

Initially the Imperial Trans-Antarctic Expedition seemed to provide a remedy that would offer Shackleton redemption. The race to the South Pole was over. The deaths of Scott and his colleagues had, in some strange and tragic way, wiped that slate clean. The expedition across the continent was something fresh, free of politics and insecurities.

The proposal that there should be two ships on this expedition led immediately to problems of manning. Thanks to Shackleton's name and profile, there were some 5000 volunteers, including the 'three sporty girls' who failed to see why 'men should have all the glory'.

In February 1914, with war daily more imminent, he contacted the Admiralty about the possibility of having one vessel manned from the Royal Navy. This ship would sail to the Ross Sea and land a party to establish relay stations for the transcontinental group.

'For this purpose,' he wrote, 'I would ask for the loan of three executive officers and 15 to 20 men. The ship will not be wintering in the Antarctic and therefore in the event of war these men would not be far away from touch with civilisation for more than three months and could immediately return to their duties if necessary.'

The Admiralty was unhelpful. Another trip south was not high on their list of priorities. Eventually they allowed one man, Captain T. Orde-Lees, to join the expedition. This decision undermined Shackleton's plan. He'd hoped that the Royal Navy would help remove the financial onus from him. Obviously, this was not going to happen.

While negotiations went on with the Admiralty, Shackleton chose a New Zealander, Frank Worsley, as captain of his own ship, the *Endurance*. Like Shackleton, Worsley had worked his way through the ranks and was to become a close friend.

In choosing his second and third mates, Shackleton opted for the Irishman Tom Crean and Alfred Cheetham, men who already knew the Antarctic and the demands of life there. Cheetham had already served on the *Morning* (the ship sent in support of the *Discovery*), the *Nimrod* and the *Terra Nova*. Crean, an able seaman in the Royal Navy from Annascaul, County Kerry, had been on the *Discovery* and *Terra Nova* expeditions with Scott.

The threat of war meant that many of the men Shackleton might have hoped to recruit were unavailable. The bulk of his crew was drawn from former merchant seamen now working on trawlers. Lionel Greenstreet, the navigating officer, was called in as a late replacement, getting the news the day before the *Endurance* sailed.

When it came to the shore party, the men with whom he would share the rigours of the expedition, Shackleton had already recruited Frank Wild, and together they discussed who they would take.

From Cambridge, Shackleton recruited the geologist James Wordie. George Marston was employed as expedition artist. Another Cambridge man was the physicist Reginald James.

James experienced one of those inimitable Shackleton interviews:

Tom Crean and Alf Cheetham (below). Tom Crean (1877-1938) later opened The South Pole Inn in Anascaul, County Kerry, Ireland. He is buried in a family tomb he built himself at Ballynacourty. Alf Cheetham served on four expeditions to the Antarctic. He was torpedoed and drowned off the Humber estuary in 1918.

'I ... was appointed after an interview of about ten minutes at the outside, probably more nearly five ... he asked if my teeth were good, if I suffered from varicose veins, if I had a good temper, and if I could sing ... he said: "O, I don't mean any Caruso stuff; but I suppose you can shout a bit with the boys?" He then asked if my circulation was good. I said it was except for one finger, which frequently went dead in cold weather. He asked me if I would seriously mind losing it. I said I would risk that. He did not ask me about my physics ... After this he put out his hand and said: "Very well, I'll take you." '

Leonard Hussey, an anthropologist, physicist and meteorologist, was told to bring his banjo; Shackleton confided to him that he had chosen him because he thought he 'looked funny'.

Another example of a what made Shackleton select a man occurred when he was interviewing a surgeon, Alexander Macklin. Noticing that Macklin wore spectacles, Shackleton asked why. Macklin's reply, 'Many a wise face would look foolish without spectacles', caught Shackleton's fancy and he took him on.

It might seem that Shackleton was flippant, careless even, in choosing his comrades, but this hail-fellow-well-met attitude was simply a camouflage. Long before the pleasantries, he had done his research on the men's expertise. The final interviews provided a check on their social skills, their ease in getting on with others, the talents they might bring in music or entertainment or sheer good humour, qualities not to be underestimated on an expedition. Faith in a man was something Shackleton valued. He expected loyalty, but also believed in giving it. More than most, he knew what exactly was important in Antarctica.

Frank Hurley, the expedition photographer, had just returned from the Antarctic with Douglas Mawson, Australia's greatest polar explorer. Shackleton wanted him on the trip and wired him in Australia, inviting him to join the ship. Hurley immediately agreed.

Thus, man by man, the *Endurance* team was drawn together.

In the early summer of 1914 Shackleton left crewing concerns behind and travelled to Norway to test the propeller-powered sledge that he hoped would make life easier on the ice. Eight of the *Endurance* party went with him and they treated the trip as a dress rehearsal for the southern adventure. The all-important sledges worked, though Shackleton thought the engines needed to be stronger to pull the weights expected.

Frank Hurley
(1885-1962),
a professional and
determined Australian
photographer who
accompanied the
Endurance expedition,
his second trip to the
Antarctic; he took at
least eight cameras
including two
cinecameras. His
father advised him as
a young boy, 'Find a
way or make one for
yourself.'

During the Norwegian stay, the team also tested the rations they would take. Shackleton was conscious as ever of the need for food that gave sustenance, and got the advice of the nutritionist Wilfred Beveridge. He also believed that a mixed diet of fresh meat where possible and tinned food where necessary would keep scurvy at bay. Charles Green, the cook who travelled on the *Endurance*, was to prove more than capable of looking after the dietary needs of the men.

Back in London preparations continued. Interestingly the *Endurance* was one of the first expedition vessels to be insured for her time in the ice floes. Until then ships were only insured to their last port of call before entering the ice. The hull and machinery were insured for £10,000. The premium was £665. An article in *The Times* noted that 'recent records of Antarctic navigation contain no instance of disaster that could be covered by insurance'.

Meanwhile, visitors to the ship, then on the Thames, were many and varied. Some paid for the pleasure, the money going towards the expedition. Others, like Queen Alexandra and Empress Marie of Russia, attended in their official capacities. During her visit on 16 July, the queen presented Shackleton with two Bibles, a Union Jack and a silk replica of her personal Royal Standard.

By the time the *Endurance* left London, on 1 August, war was no longer just a possibility. Two days later there was a general mobilization and Shackleton immediately offered the services of the *Endurance* to the Admiralty. When this was turned down, on the basis that the expedition was so far advanced that the money committed would be wasted, he offered his own services to the king, who advised him to continue. Even then, he was loath to opt out of the coming fight and, after the *Endurance* had sailed, continued to seek reassurance that he should follow her. Only at the end of August did he convince himself to go south and accepted that, while men aplenty were available to fight, few could do his job.

Three weeks later, on 27 September, he travelled to Buenos Aires to join the *Endurance*. Even then he was troubled, not by the war he was leaving but by unresolved financial and personal problems. As ever, there was enough money to get on with the current plan but the inevitability of a shortfall to come.

Endurance *leaving Buenos Aires 26 October 1914. There were three new crew on board, Charlie Green the cook, Wiliam Bakewell, an American pretending to be a Canadian, and a ninteen-year-old stowaway, Perce Blackborow.*

On a personal level Shackleton was haunted by the might-have-beens of life. He wrote to Emily bemoaning their parting: 'I don't want to go away into the South with any mis-understanding between us: I know that if you were married to a more domesticated man you would have been much happier and I also suppose I am just obsessed with my work … just now my nerves are all on edge … I could hardly have pulled through those last two months without a breakdown.'

The co-dependence between Emily and Shackleton surfaces in the letter. He wanted to travel but could only go with her support, and the unhappiness between them was now causing discomfort. He needed to be away, but needed her benediction.

Later, he would write to her pointing out he loved 'the fight and when things [are] easy I hate it … I don't think I will ever go on a long expedition again.'

He was also aware of the constant financial pressure he was putting them under: 'Money is the most useful thing,' he wrote. For years he had been struggling to find money, believing that being best would bring the reward of security. Yet there were no firsts or bests to show for his work, nothing that would guarantee his place or his income.

Travelling south, with time on his hands, guilt preyed constantly on his mind. Once he joined the *Endurance*, work and the pressures he enjoyed, the physical and mental challenges of the expedition, took over. On 16 October the *Endurance* sailed from Buenos Aires and the expedition was officially underway.

A few days out from port, a young stowaway called Perce Blackborow was discovered and taken to Shackleton. Blackborow had tried to join the *Endurance* and, being told she

Perce Blackborow, discovered stowed away after leaving Buenos Aires, he was made a steward. On 16 June 1916 the toes of his left foot were amputated on Elephant Island. After the war he worked with his father in Newport docks in Wales. Died 1949. On his shoulder, Mrs Chippy, expedition carpenter Henry McNeish's cat, a champion mouser who 'routinely monitored the ship's furnaces and stores'.

was sufficiently crewed, had decided to take his fate into his hands. Shackleton gave him a dressing down before signing him on, telling the nineteen-year-old: 'And if anyone has to be eaten, you will be the first.' At South Georgia, which the *Endurance* reached in early November, supplies and coal were taken on. During this period he made two decisions – one practical, the other a characteristic flight of money-making fancy. The first was that he would over-winter the *Endurance* and make his attempt at crossing the continent the following summer. The other was to establish a whaling company when he got back to England. He reckoned the profits could run to as much as £50,000 a year.

Within a few days of leaving South Georgia, the first of the troubles the *Endurance* was to face began. The Norwegian whaling men had warned Shackleton that conditions in the Weddell Sea were particularly bad that season. As Blackborow recounted in a lecture many years later: 'Actually, we met the pack on our second day out. This was very disturbing for our leader, for although he had been warned by the whalers of bad ice conditions he had expected a little better than this.' Shackleton himself described this as a 'gigantic jigsaw' of solid ice and open water that froze and smoked. At times the ice could be rammed but at other times the blocks were such that ramming was dangerous. It was more a question of the ship chasing her tail, winding through the pack-ice and moving slowly when she moved at all. The longer the time, the greater the concern about the coal supplies being eaten up by ice-floe delays where open water might have been expected.

Christmas Day, like the days before, was one of slow progress. Shackleton, as ever, ensured it was celebrated, with presents for the men and, as Worsley described it, a fine dinner of 'turtle soup, whitebait, jugged hare, Xmas puddg. Fired with brandy in approved style, mince pies, dates, figs, crystallised fruit &c. rum and stout for drinks … Party and singsong in evening.'

The cat-and-mouse chase between ship and ice continued over the following five days until the *Endurance* crossed the Antarctic Circle on the second-last day of the year.

Twenty-four hours later she was firmly wedged between two floes and pushed six degrees over. Only by anchoring and pulling on chains was the crew able to free her from this trap.

In the first week of January 1915 the crew took the opportunity to bring the dogs out on the ice floe for exercise while the men played football. At the end of the week, a break in the ice allowed the ship to make a hundred miles in open water and, by 15 January she was in a bay that seemed to offer shelter for the winter. Shackleton, however, decided to push farther south. It was to be a decision of enormous consequence, and one he would regret.

By the end of the third week in January the ship was again caught in ice and, to save coal, Shackleton ordered that the boilers be let go out. For a week he lived in the faint hope that the *Endurance* might float out of trouble.

Echoes of a previous experience in Antarctica were beginning to haunt him. The ship was jammed twenty-five miles short of his chosen landing-site and it looked as though she wouldn't get any closer before the following spring. Finally, on 24 February, Shackleton told the crewmen that the current position would be their wintering station. He had little choice.

With the boilers no longer working, there was no heat and less comfort on the ship. The cabins were bitterly cold, so new quarters were built by the carpenter, and the men moved into more bearable surroundings.

Once the wintering regime was established, the transcontinental group began working with the dogs. Each of the six men chosen – Shackleton, Crean, Wild, Hurley, Macklin and Marston – would have a team of seven dogs at his disposal. There would be no repetition of previous experiences; the dogs and their drivers would be well prepared.

Even though it seemed likely that the *Endurance* would return to South Georgia for a spring refit, before making another attempt at the crossing, Shackleton was adamant that the time on the ice was used to good effect. The ship might be frozen in but work must go on.

Apart from work, there was the usual winter entertainment and amusements. Books were available from the ship's library. Singing contests gave way to a bad singing contest, and Shackleton was voted a clear winner. In a mass haircutting all the men had their heads

Endurance fast in sea
ice, February 1915.
shaved to the bone. Discussions and debates were constants, and slide-shows and mock trials proved very popular.

As on previous expeditions, Shackleton encouraged the men to take exercise and keep fit. Hurley erected electric lights on and around the ship so that they could walk safely on the floe.

The unchanging soundtrack for the *Endurance* crew through that winter was the noise of

Some hope. EHS inspecting lead in ice, October 1915, shortly before they had to abandon ship.

On deck of Endurance, end of winter 1915, showing dog kennels made from boxes.

the ice shifting and sighing. The ship, however, seemed safe enough and, on midwinter's day, 22 June, the crew organized a celebration which involved three full and appetizing meals followed by speeches, songs and sketches.

As the weeks passed, the ice tightened around the ship but nothing suggested that she wouldn't be free come spring.

October, however, brought a build in the ice pressure and by the 18th of the month the ship had tilted at an angle of thirty degrees. Added to the constant creaking of the ice and groaning of the ship's timbers was the sound of the terrified dogs howling. A week later the *Endurance* was leaking and Shackleton gave orders that provisions and equipment be moved onto the floe. Taking what they could, the men descended onto the ice, to be greeted by a chorus of eight Emperor penguins, which sang what sounded like a lament.

On 27 October Hurley recorded in his diary: 'Closer and closer the ice wave approaches … Now it is within a few yards of the vessel … We … can only look impotently on … All hands are ordered to stand by to discharge equipment and stores onto the ice … The ship is doomed.'

And doomed she was. That night the men tried to sleep on the floe but sleep was impossible. Perce Blackborow would recall that 'our little ship was finally overwhelmed and

*Endurance
in ice,1915.*

crushed … we camped on the ice with the nearest land 350 miles away. The "Boss" called us all together and told us our true position and his intention.'

The practicalities of organizing his men quickly took over from any feelings of loss Shackleton might have had. Looking back was not going to solve the problems of the present or the challenge of the immediate future. As ever in such circumstances, Shackleton was at his best.

The initial camp, about a hundred yards from the ship, had to be moved when the floe began to shatter. Once a new campsite had been chosen and the tents pitched, Shackleton called a meeting of the twenty-seven men and outlined his plan to walk to Paulet Island. Having thanked them for their calmness, he suggested they try to get some sleep. He kept watch through the night and raised the alarm around midnight as the floe began to crack again. Once more, the tents were moved to a safer place.

At dawn, Shackleton, Wild and Hurley went aboard and took petrol from the *Endurance*. They then boiled milk and brought it round to their comrades, some of whom were unimpressed, it seems, by the work that had gone into preparing the hot drink. Wild, annoyed at the nonchalance with which the gesture was received, commented wryly to some of the men: 'If any of you gentlemen would like your boots cleaned just put them outside!'

Much of that morning was spent taking what might be useful from the fractured ship. Three boats were loaded on sledges and the men packed personal belongings, being allowed no more than two pounds weight each. Shackleton took some pages from the ship's Bible but left his gold watch and several sovereigns behind. He did, however, insist that Hussey take his banjo.

On 30 October the party began its slow journey away from the *Endurance*. Given the dangerous state of the floe, Shackleton insisted the men stay together and move with as much care as possible. Heavy snow kept them on the floe in what they named Ocean Camp.

Again, Perce Blackborow remembered the men were on 'about 9 ozs food daily ration. I like to think of our leader as I recall him at this time. His hopes & ambitions had all been shattered – yet he was cheerful & went out of his way to impart some of his cheerfulness to others. He had a genius for keeping his men in good spirits, & need I say more, we loved him like a father.'

Day after day, parties went back to the ship. Nails were taken from planks and saved for future carpentry needs. Hurley and Shackleton spent hours sorting through the photographic plates, limiting what could be taken to the contents of one tin. The other plates were smashed. This was a brutal but final way of limiting the choice and avoiding second thoughts.

Life on the floe went on. Once the essentials had been established – safety and the building of a proper kitchen – the men settled into a routine. The future, whatever it might bring, was not yet an issue. Patience was the watchword.

On 21 November the packed ice temporarily broke and the men watched the *Endurance* slip to her end. Worsley wrote that she 'put up the bravest fight that ever ship had fought before yielding … Nothing is now visible of her but 20 feet of her stern pointing pitifully up to Heaven. She remains like this a few minutes & then slowly slips down beneath her icy shroud & is seen no more … .At 5 p.m. we saw her end.'

The break-up of the ice, which had swallowed the *Endurance*, also allowed for a possible escape from the floe. Knowing that it was time to move, Shackleton decided the team would celebrate Christmas Day on 22 December. A dinner of ham, hare, parsnips, baked beans, peaches, biscuits, jam and coffee or cocoa was followed by the striking of camp.

Next day Shackleton and Wild moved ahead to review the lie of the land. Worsley was left in charge. In Shackleton's absence, words passed between Worsley and Harry McNeish, the carpenter. The main party came to a halt, spectators to the stand-off. On his return, Shackleton found McNeish maintaining that the march across the ice was madness. Shackleton quickly reminded all of the men that they were still in his employ and that orders must be obeyed. In particular, he would not stand for anyone disobeying the order of an officer.

The falling-out came at a bad time. Progress was slow and Shackleton was under extreme pressure. His diary entry about McNeish was short and to the point: 'Everyone working well except the carpenter: I shall never forget him in this time of strain and stress.' Nor did he, refusing to recommend him for a Polar Medal when the expedition ended.

The initial hopes of the men – that they might make progress towards rescue – were to be stymied by the breaking ice and unstable conditions. Instead of going forward they were forced to retreat to a solid floe.

On New Year's Eve Shackleton wrote in his diary: 'May the new one bring us good fortune … Ice seems to be rotting away … I long for some rest free from thought.'

Two weeks later, knowing the boats were their only hope and that food supplies were dwindling, Shackleton ordered more of the dogs shot. Another week passed and the floe drifted back across the Antarctic Circle. Another small milestone had been reached.

Shackleton had taken two boats with him onto the floe but in early February he agreed to send a party back to bring the third boat to the camp. Until the men reappeared, he was ill at ease. Their safety was paramount to him. Sometimes, in the grip of a nightmare, his voice could be heard across the icy wilderness and, when he woke, he inevitably recounted some dream of losing men. In a strange way, his care for his men, always a priority, seemed regularly to be haunted by the ghost of his dead rival and the possibility that, but for the grace of God, he might find himself in a similar position.

Months drifted by on the ice, February moving into March without any change in the patterns of the men's lives. Late in the month their floe began to melt and to pick up speed. They sat on the ice, powerless to do anything to alter their course. On 7 April they came in sight of Clarence Island, next door to Elephant Island on which they were to land. With the sighting came the reminder that missing the island would send them out into the open ocean and God alone knew what fate. Then nature took a hand. The floe split through their camp and the following day the three boats were launched and the men began to row.

The fall of night saw them camp on another floe. During the night this floe cracked, throwing Holness into the sea. For the rest of the night, he was kept moving because there was no dry clothing for him. Walter How recalled how 'every movement he made with his legs and arms, there was a crackle of icy clothes'.

The days that followed, spent in the open boats, were terrifying. The ice floes were too dangerous to trust for camps and the boats provided little shelter. With no way of cooking, the men were reduced to eating dry dog food which brought on bouts of diarrhoea. Constantly wet from the breaking waves, constantly sick from the rough seas, the men finally got ashore on 15 April at Cape Valentine at the east end of Elephant Island.

Shackleton made an occasion of the landing, suggesting the stowaway, Blackborow, as the youngest, be first ashore. The young man, however, was badly frostbitten and, as soon as he set foot in the water at the shore, he collapsed into the waves. The men laughed emotionally, rushing to follow him, setting their feet on solid land for the first time in more than sixteen months.

Blackborow wrote of the day: 'Sir E.S. gave me the great honour of being the first man to land ... All the company had suffered severely from exposure & frostbite, several being in a very bad way.'

Two days later they were on the sea again, moving camp to a safer and more hospitable point up the coast to a beach they named Cape Wild.

Elephant Island measures 23 miles by 13 (at its widest point) and, while it offered fresh food in the form of penguins, birds and sea elephants, it was not a welcoming haven. Constant rain and snow and gale force winds meant that life there was extremely harsh. Worse still, the island was not on the regular whaling routes and the chances of their being found were slim. Shackleton decided there was only one choice in the circumstances. A boat would go for help, 800 miles to South Georgia. Wild was to take charge of the men on the island, while he led the rescue party.

McNeish set to work on the chosen boat, the *James Caird*, making a shelter and deck at the forward end of the craft. The six men chosen to crew the *James Caird* were Crean, McCarthy and Shackleton, all Irishmen, McNeish, Vincent and Worsley. On 24 April they left Elephant Island and the twenty-two men whose lives were to depend on their reaching land safely.

As Blackborow recalled, Shackleton and his crew set off on a 'desperate venture ... in a small lifeboat in an attempt to reach S. Georgia, over 800 miles away across the most tempestuous seas in the world'. By the next day, the pack ice closed in and their departure would have been impossible.

Life on the *James Caird* was precarious. Three man watches of four hours, during which each had a job – one on the tiller, one bailing, one attending to the sails - were followed by four hours off watch, when the men tried to sleep in the narrow and constantly wet confines of the boat. Cooking on board was limited to what could be done with a primus stove jammed between the feet of two men, one leaning against each side of the boat. Tom Crean was the primus expert and chef. Shackleton insisted that breakfast, lunch and an evening

James Caird *departing Point Wild on Elephant Island, 24 April 1916. The next day the bay filled with pack ice, blocking it for weeks. The* James Caird *was a 22 feet 6 inches long, double-ended, carvel-built ship's boat now on display at Shackleton's old school, Dulwich College, London.*

meal be taken at set times, the routine helping to maintain the generally high spirits of the men. Worsley described Shackleton's concern for his comrades as having 'a touch of woman'.

Each individual drew strength from the reliability of his comrades. Shackleton wrote that Crean's singing reminded him of 'the chanting of a Buddhist monk ... In moments of inspiration Crean would attempt "The Wearing of the Green".'

Icing on the boat and choppy seas made the first week and a half of the journey a trial but on 5 May difficulty gave way to danger when the boat was hit by a gale. Shackleton saw what he thought was a break in the cloud only to realize immediately that what he had imagined to be light was, in fact, the crest of a wave 'so gigantic ... a thing quite apart from the ... seas that had been our tireless enemies for many days. I shouted: "For God's sake, hold on! It's got us!" Then came a moment of suspense that seemed drawn out into hours ... We felt our boat lifted and flung forward like a cork in breaking surf ... but somehow the boat lived through it, half-full of water, sagging to the dead weight ... We baled with the energy of men fighting for life ... and after ten minutes of uncertainty we felt the boat renew her life beneath us.'

The following day the sun put in a brief appearance, as though to check they were still afloat and alive. During the voyage, Worsley's four readings using sextant and sun were vital for keeping them on the right course for South Georgia.

The next problem was a shortage of water. One of the containers had been damaged and contaminated with seawater. Rations were cut to a half-pint per man per day.

8 May, however, brought a sight that lifted their spirits and gave them new energy. Just after midday McCarthy sighted a cliff face, and they realized that they were close to South Georgia.

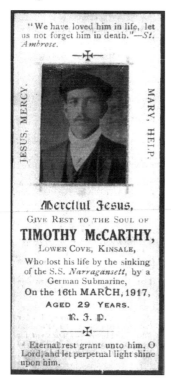

" We have loved him in life, let us not forget him in death."—*St. Ambrose.*

JESUS, MERCY.   MARY, HELP.

Merciful Jesus,

GIVE REST TO THE SOUL OF

TIMOTHY McCARTHY,

LOWER COVE, KINSALE,

Who lost his life by the sinking of the S.S. *Narragansett*, by a German Submarine,

On the 16th MARCH, 1917,

AGED 29 YEARS.

R. 3. P.

Eternal rest grant unto him, O Lord, and let perpetual light shine upon him.

Tim McCarthy's Mass card. Born Kinsale, County Cork, Ireland, where there are now memorials to him and his brother Mortimer. Chosen for the James Caird boat journey, he was highly thought of by Shackleton and Worsley for his great cheerfulness and optimism. Died 1917 when his ship was torpedoed in the English Channel. (Courtesy Terry Connolly)

The following day, in the teeth of a gale, they worked their way clear of rocks and on 10 May finally got ashore, landing by chance at the mouth of a freshwater stream. A stew of young albatross and Bovril formed their first hot and sustaining meal in over two weeks.

Shackleton planned to take the boat farther up the coast to find a better site for a camp and then set off on foot across the island for help. There was one problem: the rudder of the *James Caird* had been lost in the rough seas that took them in. Miraculously it seemed, on 13 May the rudder was washed up at the exact spot where they were camped. Repairs were made and two days later they were back at sea, working along the difficult coast until they found a safer place to land and a point from which Crean, Shackleton and Worsley would walk to Stromness in search of help. McCarthy was to look after McNeish and Vincent who were suffering from exposure.

At 3 a.m. on 19 May the three set off, ill clothed and ill equipped for the journey ahead, forced to use an adze as an ice-pick, carrying their equipment in bundles like schoolboys. Climbing to find their bearings, they discovered that their chart, no more than an outline of the island, was less than accurate. Time after time, they climbed only to be met by cliffs and forced back down again. The most immediate danger was the prospect of being caught at altitude without sleeping-bags or any proper protection from the bitter cold.

As darkness fell, the men cut ice-steps down the side of one cliff and then, peering through the darkness, they imagined the ground sloped away more gently. But between fog and blackness they couldn't be sure. Shackleton made a decision to risk sledging down, using their rope as a protection from snow burn.

Sitting one behind the other on the coiled rope, Shackleton then Worsley then Crean, the three pushed themselves forward, not knowing where they were going or what lay ahead.

Worsley described the sensation: 'I was never more scared in my life than for the first thirty seconds. The speed was terrific. I think we all gasped at the hair-raising shoot into the darkness … Then, to our joy, the slope curved out and we shot into a bank of soft snow. We estimated we had shot down a mile in two or three minutes and had lowered our altitude by two or three thousand feet. We stood up and shook hands.'

To Shackleton's amusement, Worsley had lost most of the backside of his trousers in their trip down the mountain. Turning around, however, he discovered that he was in a similar state himself.

Pushing on, dehydrated and exhausted, they were forced to stop for rest and sleep. The three huddled together for whatever passed for warmth, and Worsley and Crean slept. Fearing hypothermia and death, Shackleton stayed awake. He allowed the pair to sleep for what he said was half an hour. Afterwards, he would admit he had only let them sleep for five minutes before waking them and moving on.

Walking across the bleak island, under an intense full moon, the men walked down until, on the morning of 20 May they saw the sight they hardly dared imagine, the glimmering waters of Stromness Bay. Behind them lay months of pain and hunger and doubt, ahead lay twelve miles of difficult terrain but only twelve miles. Their hearts soared and their energy seemed suddenly restored.

As they made breakfast, Shackleton heard a steam-whistle cutting the white silence of the landscape. 'Never had any of us heard sweeter music,' he wrote. 'It was the first sound created by outside human agency that had come to our ears since we left Stromness Bay in December 1914.'

It was half-past one that afternoon when the three figures stumbled over the crest of a ridge and saw below them men and ships, life and hope. Again, they shook hands and moved down towards the harbour.

The full realization of how they looked hit home in the late afternoon when, as they reached the outskirts of the whaling station, two small boys ran away terrified at the sight. An old man directed them to the station manager's office.

A man named Mansell watched as the three came in. Later, he would describe the scene.

'Everybody at Stromness knew Shackleton well, and we very sorry he is lost in ice with all hands. But we do not know three terrible-looking bearded men who walk into the office off the mountainside … Manager say: "Who the hell are you" and terrible bearded man in the centre of the three say very quietly: "My name is Shackleton." Me – I turn away and weep. I think manager weep too.'

Later, Shackleton would look back on the journey and write: 'We had "suffered, starved and triumphed, grovelled down yet grasped at glory, grown bigger in the bigness of the

Whaling manager's house, Stromness, South Georgia. Shackleton, Crean and Worsley arrived there 20 May 1916 after crossing South Georgia. They were welcomed by the amazed manager, Thoraff Sorlle, and that evening had their first baths for six months. This historic building still stands.

whole". We had seen God in his splendours, heard the text that Nature renders. We had reached the naked soul of man.'

His use of strong spiritual language in recounting how the journey across South Georgia affected him is hardly surprising. In time, Worsley and Crean and he would all refer to the fact that, as they crossed the high whiteness, they felt, constantly, that there was a fourth person present. None spoke of the feeling to the others. Shackleton recounts in his book *South* how Worsley said to him: '"Boss. I had a curious feeling on the march that there was another person with us." ' Crean confessed to the same idea. One feels ' "the dearth of human words, the roughness of mortal speech" in trying to describe things intangible'.

The echoes of Luke 24:13–16 are unmistakable. 'And, behold, two of them went that same day to a village called Emmaus ... And it came to pass, that, while they communed together and reasoned, Jesus himself drew near, and went with them. But their eyes were holden that they should not know him.'

Whatever happened on that journey, collectively and individually, none of the three would ever forget the sensation of the other, the absent friend who was with them to the end and only left when they were safely delivered.

As soon as Shackleton had organized for a whaler, the *Samson*, Worsley boarded it and travelled back to pick up the three men on the other side of the island. Shackleton and Crean went on to Husvik and arranged that the *Southern Sky* be pressed into service to try to reach Elephant Island. Ingvar Thom, an old acquaintance of Shackleton's, agreed to captain her. He also arranged a get-together on his ship, the *Orwell*, where a large gathering of sailors and whaling men met to honour Shackleton and his comrades. Worsley described the scene: 'One spoke in Norse, and the manager translated. He said he had been at sea over forty years; that he knew this stormy Southern Ocean intimately ... and that never had he heard of such a wonderful feat of daring seamanship as bringing the 22-ft open boat from Elephant Island to South Georgia, and then, to crown it, tramping across the ice and snow and rocky heights of the interior, and that he felt it an honour to meet and shake hands with Sir Ernest and his comrades. He finished with the dramatic words: "These are men!"'

The *Southern Sky* left for Elephant Island on 23 May but she was only three days out when they met ice and, though she got within seventy miles of the island, there was no way through. Instead, Shackleton took her on to the Falklands, to get word of their plight to the wider world and to send news of his survival to Emily.

'It was Nature against us the whole time' was his succinct way of describing what the men had been through and what those on Elephant Island were still enduring.

His wired appeals for help to the Admiralty and to South American countries brought a first response from the Uruguayans who offered a trawler. Shackleton, whom the Uraguayans dubbed 'el héroe irlandés', accepted immediately and on 10 June he set off on the boat, the *Instituto de Pesca No. 1*, and three days later came in sight of Elephant Island but was driven back by the ice.

Forced to return to the Falklands, Shackleton, Crean and Worsley then travelled on to Chile and secured the use of a wooden schooner, the *Emma*, and a small steel steam tug, the *Yelcho*. On 12 July they set out again but bad weather drove them back. Typically, he wrote home frequently to his family. On 1 August he told his elder son Raymond, 'I am writing this on the way up from the ice, we have just made another attempt to rescue the men on Elephant Island but our little schooner was not strong enough … I know you will be a great help and comfort to Mummy by working well at school and looking after her when at home, she is a mother in a million as I know you must already realize and she has not had an easy time of it and there has been much sadness. God Bless you. Your loving, wandering father.'

Stranded in Port Stanley on 8 August, Shackleton waited for word from the Admiralty. Despite his impatience, he realized that war and distance were impediments to help from Britain. Wires from London informed him that the *Discovery* would be sent when she had finished being repaired and that he should rest up in Port Stanley. This was not what he wanted to hear. Again, the Chilean government came to his assistance. Taking the *Yelcho* alone, and promising not to risk her in the ice, he left Punta Arenas on 25 August and reached Elephant Island five days later.

At first, the men on the island feared the ship was passing them by. They had no way of knowing Shackleton was aboard. A fire was lit but by then the ship was making for them. Soon, a rowing boat was seen on the waves, Shackleton standing in it, enquiring across the water if they were all well. The twenty-two men could only stare.

Shackleton was greeted by a crew who had always tried to believe he would return for them. They were also men who had been pushed to the limits of their physical and psychological being, living under the two remaining upturned ship's boats. They were hungry and exhausted, in some instances living on the brink of madness. Frank Wild's calm leadership has seen them through. Shackleton he had done what he promised: he had come back for his comrades, and taken them to safety.

In October 1916 Shackleton wrote a letter to his agent Ernest Perris explaining he was 'dead tired and very lonely'. However, he went on to pen short, candid reports on each of the crew members: 'I know these men's hearts,' he wrote, and he did.

Back in Punta Arenas, Shackleton wrote in the visitors' book of the Spanish Consul lines by St John Lucas. They said more than he might ever have managed or dared to say about those he despised, those he respected, those he loved, and about himself:

> 'We were the fools who could not rest
> In the dull earth we left behind,
> And burned with passion for the south
> And drank strange frenzy from its wind.
> The world where wise men sit at ease
> Fades from our unregretful eyes,
> And thus across uncharted seas,
> We stagger on our enterprise.'

While this drama of survival had been played out on one side of Antartica, another was being played out on the other. The *Aurora* crew, charged with laying supplies on the Ross Ice Shelf for the transcontinental team, had, after financial problems kept them in Australia six weeks longer than intendeded, gone about their work. Again, not all went as planned.

Having landed shore crews and been anchored as a winter base, the ship was torn from her moorings in early May 1915 and left drifting with the ice, unable to make contact with either the ten men who had been stranded or with potential rescuers.

By 2 June the two parties left on the ice – one laying depots, the other engaged in scientific work – had reconnoitred at Cape Evans and prepared for the winter. Available supplies, while not what they would have chosen, ensured no one would starve.

The major problem was the surfeit of chiefs in the party. Aeneas Mackintosh was in

charge, theoretically, but neither Ernest Joyce nor Fred Stevens, the chief scientist, had much faith in Mackintosh, blaming him for the fact that men had been allowed to come ashore without adequate supplies in the event of an emergency. Furthermore, they blamed him for the positioning of the ship which, they believed, had led to her being blown out of reach by the storms. Their views on Shackleton also differed. Joyce was blindly loyal, Stevens was unimpressed by the planning – or lack of it – that Shackleton had put into the *Aurora*. The forced companionship of the moment was unavoidable, but it did nothing to ease the tensions between the men.

At the beginning of September, three ill-equipped parties of three set off to lay further depots, leaving Stevens to continue his scientific research alone at Cape Evans. Initially, and through the sheer hard work of the men, the depot laying went well. As there were few dogs left, the men were forced to pull loads of between 150 and 200 pounds each. Such was their determination to keep their promise to Shackleton, they worked willingly despite the continuing bickering of Mackintosh and Joyce. The arguments often revolved around the benefits of using dogs rather than man-hauling. Joyce had a way with dogs, Macintosh had little time for them. The root of the problem lay in the fact that neither Joyce nor Mackintosh regarded the other as a suitable leader.

On 3 January 1916, with one of the primus stoves no longer working, three of the men on the depot-laying trek were sent back to Cape Evans. A week later Mackintosh swallowed his pride and asked Joyce to take over as leader of a joint party. There were now six men left on the journey – Joyce, Mackintosh, Hayward, Richards, Spencer-Smith and Wild.

In the days that followed both Mackintosh and Spencer-Smith became ill and, although Joyce suggested turning back, Mackintosh emphatically refused. Whether his refusal was a sign of his intention to complete the job he had told Shackleton he would do or whether, having given up on the leadership, he was now refusing to bend to Joyce's control a second time is a moot point.

On 22 January Spencer-Smith was left behind with a fortnight's supplies, while the other five went on. Finally, on 26 January a depot was laid at the Beardmore Glacier. They had achieved what they set out to do.

Turning for base that day, the men recognized the dangers that lay ahead. Mackintosh's knee was severely swollen, Joyce was partially snow-blind, and all five were suffering from scurvy.

On 29 January they reached Spencer-Smith to find him too ill to walk. Putting him on a sledge they moved on again. Mackintosh's knee was now so badly swollen that he could barely walk but he refused to be put on a sledge and so the ragged band continued, moving painfully slowly through the snow, undernourished and suffering from exposure.

By 23 February the men were so weak that they could no longer pull Spencer-Smith on the sledge and he and Mackintosh were left behind with Wild to look after them. So weak

Mackintosh and Rev. Spencer-Smith on sledge, February–March 1916. Spencer-Smith, who knew Charlie Green, met Shackleton in Buenos Aires and was taken on as photographer on the Ross Sea party. The first cleric in Antarctica, Spencer-Smith died 9 March 1916. Mackintosh was last seen setting out over sea ice to the hut at Cape Evans with Hayward on 8 May.

was Spencer-Smith that he couldn't leave his sleeping-bag and Wild had the unenviable task of looking after his hygiene.

Joyce, Richards and Hayward went on. A blizzard forced them to camp, even though they were out of food and reduced to eating dog food and letting the dogs go without. The shadow of Scott fell over Joyce. Constantly mindful of what had happened to Scott and his men, he was determined he and his comrades would not suffer a similar fate. Somehow the three moved on, taking two hours to cover a distance of three-quarters of a mile, and finally reached the depot on 26 February. They were exhausted, ill and starving, faint mirror images of the trio who would later stagger into a whaling station on South Georgia.

Three days on, somewhat resuscitated, they arrived back with supplies for Mackintosh, Spencer-Smith and Wild. Wild, hearing the dogs, staggered from the tent, his sledge harness already on, and, despite his hunger and weakness, coming to help pull the sledge.

The party set off again only to have Hayward fall ill. There was nothing for it but to put the two sickest men, Mackintosh and Spencer-Smith on sledges and to pull them. And this is what was done. Joyce, Richards and Wild dragged their human cargo over the soft snow, hardly able to move but determined to continue. Hayward staggered along as well as he could.

A week of this punishing routine saw them reach breaking-point. They simply didn't have the energy to go on and Mackintosh volunteered to be temporarily left behind.

On 9 March, while the men lay in their tent, Spencer-Smith died. He had been particularly ill through the night, complaining of chest pains and cold. The temperature was – 30 degrees. At six in the morning he stopped breathing.

Forty-eight hours later the four men reached Hut Point and on 16 March they returned for Mackintosh and brought him safely back to the hut.

Poignantly, Joyce would later recount how, even in the worst of times, he would look over his shoulder somehow hoping he might catch sight of Shackleton and his five companions gaining on them out of the blizzard. But an extraordinary undertaking had been completed: they had walked almost 1600 miles, over 200 days, with little to eat, poorly equipped, eventually sacrificing a life, but they had laid the depots as promised for a leader who would never reach them.

The unpredictability of the ice meant the men were forced to remain at Hut Point into early May. Mackintosh in particular was anxious to get back to Cape Evans to discover whether there was any news of the *Aurora*. The others were less inclined to move, fearing danger on the unstable ice. On 7 May, despite warnings from his comrades, Mackintosh insisted that he was moving and the following day he and Hayward set off, promising to return if they ran into trouble. The pair left the hut at 1 p.m. Two hours later a blizzard swept across the landscape, engulfing everything. Such was the ferocity of the storm that it was two days before the men trapped inside the hut could even begin to search for Mackintosh and Hayward.

What they found, when the weather cleared, were the tracks of the pair's footsteps on the ice. They followed the trail for two miles until it ended in broken ice.

There was the slight possibility that Mackintosh and Hayward had got across before the ice broke but it was a faint hope and one that was finally dashed two months later, when Joyce and his men reached Cape Evans to discover that neither Mackintosh nor Hayward had made it.

It was to be late December 1916 before a relief ship – the *Aurora* – set out to rescue the men from Cape Evans. Shackleton had, by then, gone through protracted and excruciating negotiations with the governments of Australia and New Zealand to organize the rescue. The lack of proper financial management in the original fitting of the *Aurora* meant that Shackleton was viewed as less than reliable by both governments. Neither was willing to give command of a ship they had overhauled and underwritten to a man who appeared so blasé with other people's money. Shackleton, on the other hand, was adamant that the stranded men were his responsibility and he was the one who would rescue them. He also insisted that the *Aurora* was his ship and he wasn't about to hand her over to anyone – debts or no debts.

Eventually, a compromise was reached and Shackleton sailed on the *Aurora* under a government appointee. His position on the ship wasn't an issue with Shackleton, he simply wanted to get to his men, and he was quite content to sail out of Port Chalmers on 20 December under the command of Captain John Davis, a man of Irish descent.

Three weeks later the *Aurora* reached Cape Royds. Shackleton described the scene:

'*No sign of life at my old hut. We fired a distress signal no sign of life at Cape Evans hut. I went alone to our hut and found there a note unsigned dated Dec. 15. 1915 stating that the party was housed at Cape Evans. There was no statement as to the safety of all hands ... on looking round I noticed Wilds name and Jacks in paint that was still wet. As the two men were on the Barrier party they were the ones we were most anxious about.'*

At Cape Evans, Richards, seeing the *Aurora*, told Joyce: 'Their shouts of "Ship ho!" brought their comrades running and they shook each other by the hand, all worries and troubles passed overboard.'

After reuniting with his comrades, and learning that Mackintosh and Hayward were missing, Shackleton organized a search party, but no trace of the pair was found. Before leaving the ice, a cross was erected in memory of Mackintosh, Hayward and Spencer-Smith, and Shackleton had lines from Browning's 'Prospice' buried with the names of the three men, in a container beneath the cross (this container was rediscovered in 1947 by an American expedition):

> *'I was ever a fighter, so – one fight more,*
> *The best and the last!'*

So the quotation from Browning began, and so the memories of the three were commemorated by those who had miraculously survived on both sides of the continent. Shackleton had indeed met his men again, but under circumstances none could have wished or imagined.

9

Shackleton and the Great War

1917–1921

---◆---

Two and a half years had passed since Shackleton left England, and still the Great War raged across Europe. Antarctica had brought its own wars, defeats and victories and Shackleton now felt it was time to get back to England to the unfinished business of that other war. He was still as keen to fight for his country as he had been in 1914.

First were the practicalities of finishing the business of the expedition with visits to New Zealand and Australia. From New Zealand he wrote to Emily, talking of his fight against 'great odds and extraordinary conditions' of the previous years and about the 'feeling of power that I like' in the work in Antarctica. It was as if he felt a need to justify his own experiences in the face of the carnage in Europe.

Moving to Australia, he faced a barrage of criticism about the loose ends that had surrounded the *Aurora*. The broad consensus on the Australian relief committee was that he had been slovenly in his approach. Shackleton lost no time in telling the committee that he and his men had been 'treated unfairly' when they needed help. He pointed out that it was South American governments, which had come to the rescue. Australia and New Zealand, he maintained, had done little more than thwart him personally. The relief committee members were taken aback but as they listened they were impressed by Shackleton's conviction and what had seemed destined to be a difficult meeting ended with handshakes all round and an apology from the Australians.

On 20 March Shackleton addressed 11,000 people in Sydney. The crowd had come to see a hero and he didn't disappoint them. His subject was patriotism:

'To take your part in this war is not a matter merely of patriotism, not a matter merely of duty or of expediency; it is a matter of the saving of a man's soul and of a man's own opinion of himself ... We lived long dark days in the South. The danger of the moment is a thing easy to meet, and the courage of the moment is in every man at some time. But I want to say to you that we lived through slow dead days of toil, of struggle, dark striving and anxiety; days that called not for heroism in the bright light of day, but simply for dogged persistent endeavour to do what the soul said was right. It is in the same spirit that we men of the British race have to face this war. What does the war mean to Australia? Everything. It means as much to you as though the enemy was actually beating down your gate. This summons to fight is a call imperative to the manhood within you ... For this call to fight means to men more than ease, more than money, more than love of woman, more even than duty; it means the chance to prove ourselves the captains of our own soul.'

Potent as Shackleton's words were, they were as much about his own view of life as they were about the war effort. The ideals of heroism, patriotism and fighting the good fight were the same that had driven him south. The concept of looking into your soul and finding a personal truth by which to steer had long been part of his credo.

Leaving Australia, Shackleton travelled to San Francisco on the first leg of his journey back to England. There he was offered an extensive lecture tour of the United States. He turned it down, saying he wanted to be home again and settled, instead, for a month. Following a heart-warming welcome in San Francisco, he set off on a short lecture trip. In Tacoma he reduced his fee to avoid a loss to the woman who had organized the lecture. The sole advertising she had done, according to Shackleton, was to hire 'a boozy looking old man carrying a banner, evidently from some fancy dress performance they had once, covered with white cotton wool to represent snow ... He was leaning up against a lamppost covered with cotton wool.' Better moments came at well-attended lectures in New York and Chicago, arranged by the American Geographical Society.

In England Emily awaited her husband's return with some trepidation. She had long ago recognized that suburban life was not for him: 'I know it would bore Ernest to be here for any length of time – but the children have been very happy ... I only hope he will get something to do – that will interest him – as he could never be happy in a quiet domestic life.'

Shackleton himself was adamant that his presence in England would make a difference to the war effort. He had done what he could in terms of raising morale in New Zealand and Australia. Now he could hardly wait to become part of the war machine. The adventure of Antarctica was behind him, the challenge of the war lay ahead. By this time, thirty of his comrades were fighting and one, Tim MacCarthy, was dead.

When he reached England in late May he was summoned to Buckingham Palace to see the king and to give an account of the expedition. That done, he set about tidying up outstanding business. He also spent time getting to know his children again, eager to make up for lost time. But the details of domesticity were a mystery to him. Returning from an expedition where survival depended on discipline, he found the relaxed attitude to authority that Emily had encouraged in the children impossible to understand. Used to dealing with men who obeyed his commands without questioning, he became agitated with children who ignored or challenged him. Emily acted as a buffer – trying to explain her thinking to him and pointing out that she was the one who had had to deal with the day-to-day details of the children's lives and this was her way of doing it.

To add to his dissatisfaction, the possibility of an office job in London, co-ordinating food supplies for the Allies, proved less than appealing. The thought of a desk job was off-putting and he saw that 'in some quarters (it might) be thought I was avoiding the active side of the war'.

He spent much of his time in London, a compromise which suited Emily and himself. From there he could be the loving, concerned and absent father and husband, writing and telephoning to see that all was well. And from there he could continue his friendship with the actress Rosalind Chetwynd who, as Rosa Lynd, was then on the London stage. She lived in Park Lane where Shackleton was a regular visitor. He and Rosalind had first met more

EHS in North Russia in 1918: 'A sailor dressed up as a soldier.'

than a decade earlier, when she was a neighbour of Frank Shackleton. Their relationship, though interrupted by his expeditions, had continued and now that Shackleton was back in London the pair met regularly.

Photographs of Shackleton taken after his return from Antarctica and over the following three years show a man growing prematurely old. His health was a factor in this decline but there's something else in the face and the figure, signs of a man going to seed. The face is a disappointed one. In an age when victory was quintessential, he was a man who had never quite managed to win.

Worst of all, while war raged about him, a war of which he wanted to be a part, he was marooned on an island of debt-paying and problem-solving for an expedition that was already over. The past was his constant companion, the future a worrying uncertainty.

Shackleton had also begun to drink. Never comfortable with alcohol, it now seemed to offer a way out of his troubles. It may have been a temporary escape, but he recognized its dangers and regularly went on the wagon.

By July he had paid all the men involved in the trans-Antarctic expedition and felt free to seek real war work. But he met with antipathy from many of those he expected to welcome his enthusiasm. Those who had been most critical of his going south at the outbreak of the war were now unwilling to make use of his expertise.

He put forward several proposals, mostly in relation to the Russian front where, he felt, his experience would be especially useful. Finally, in September 1917, he was given a job under Sir Edward Carson in the Department of Information.

Carson was a fellow-Irishman, a barrister and an Ulster Unionist MP. In the legal world his main claim to fame was his involvement in the Oscar Wilde libel trial in 1895, where he represented the Marquess of Queensberry and won. In the world of politics Carson was the leading defender of Ulster Unionism in particular and Irish Unionism in general. In 1910 he had become head of the Unionist Party. In September 1912 he was instrumental in organizing the signing of Ulster's Solemn League and Covenant, a further stand against Home Rule by almost half a million Ulster Unionists. A year later 500 delegates of the Ulster Unionist Council elected him Chairman of the Provisional Government of Ulster. With the outbreak of war he was brought into the Cabinet and now, as Minister without Portfolio, he found a use for Shackleton – the former Unionist candidate in Scotland.

He was to travel to South America and investigate German propaganda agencies there and help to spread British propaganda. His high standing in South America would, he was told, be a great help. This wasn't the work he had expected but it was work – unpaid into the bargain – and he took it.

His lack of salary he dismissed with, 'It did not matter.'

Before he left, he was summoned again by the king, this time to Sandringham, to lecture on the trans-Antarctic expedition. Shackleton had spent the previous months trying, unsuccessfully, to have Polar medals awarded to those of his comrades whom he regarded as meriting them. The Admiralty, however, was against the idea, arguing that such awards would be frivolous in a time of war. Using his sway with royalty, he now got the awards for all but four of the men – Holness, McNeish, Stephenson and Vincent – not because they were refused but because Shackleton decided none deserved a nomination. In each case, he argued, the men had not come up to the standards he demanded of his crew. For Harry McNeish, in particular, the carpenter whose work had fitted the *James Caird* against the worst excesses of a stormy sea, the decision was particularly wounding.

On 17 October Shackleton set sail for Buenos Aires via New York. Leaving home was followed by the familiar pattern of regret and a sense of wasted opportunity. He wrote to Emily:

'I was happy really happy this time when all was right between us, and now I do not feel far away though I am missing you: I think darling that you are wonderful in many ways

*and the more I think about you the more I see what a wonderful wife you have been to me:
I suppose darling that I am a funny curious sort of wanderer but take this [from] me I have
been far happier at home these last few months than ever before ... I think our children are
just sweet in all their ways and I am proud of them of each in some particular way ... I can
only tell you that I love you.'*

Shackleton had fallen in love with Emily Dorman on shore leave; he'd courted her on shore
leave; he'd married her during one of his most prolonged periods ashore and he'd lived his
life with her between expeditions. Whether this was what she had expected, it was what she
grew to accept and what she, probably, saw as the best way of keeping the marriage alive.
Shackleton's life had been one of travelling hopefully, his arrivals home were bound to be
a disappointment, and the best love he could offer was what came from afar.

*Holness, Vincent,
How, Stephenson,
Blackborow, McLeod,
possibly 22 June
1915. Holness, Vincent
and Stephenson, as
well as McNeish, were
the only Endurance
crew members not
included in the list of
Polar Medals published
in* The Times *on
16 February 1918.*

His work in South America involved him in intelligence gathering on German propaganda efforts and countering with British information. While in Buenos Aires he was ill a number of times, finding the heat unbearable. He was also fighting a tendency towards binge drinking. As it happened, his posting there was to be short and in March 1918 he was recalled to London.

The summer was spent in England and only in August was he allowed to do what he had wanted since his return from America. He was given charge of the winter equipment for the North Russian expedition. The job-description was vague but this, the authorities believed, was the best way to deal with Shackleton. His free spirit might have been an advantage in Antarctica but it was seen as a definite obstacle when it came to army life.

The north Russian campaign was one of the more complicated and least effective of the war. Russia itself was in the throes of a civil war and the British government was anxious to keep the White Russians on its side. The Revolution had seen the new Russian government make peace with the Germans early in 1918 and one of the Revolutionaries' chief problems was in bringing the remnants of the White army under control. For the British government, however, the important issue was the maintaining of a presence in north Russia and the holding of Spitsbergen.

Spitsbergen was under Norwegian control but the new Russian government was willing to support German claims to the area. For the British, Spitsbergen was a valuable watch-point on the Arctic entry to the Atlantic but they couldn't afford to send an overt military force to what was a neutral, Norwegian area. Instead, they used the cover of the Northern Exploration Company to pursue their interests. Shackleton was invited to join the company and travel to Spitsbergen as part of the venture.

Apart from its political significance, the company, in which he had been given shares as part of his employment contract, had hopes of mining gold, coal and iron in the area and, as ever, Shackleton was looking for the opportunity to make his fortune.

With his old friends Frank Wild and James McIlroy on board, Shackleton left Aberdeen for Norway early in August. Having reached Tromso, he became ill with a suspected heart attack. Despite McIlroy's offer, he refused to undergo a medical examination.

His gradual recovery coincided with his recall to London by the War Office. His new orders were to organize and accompany the shipment of equipment to Murmansk to relieve an expeditionary group, which had arrived in June. He would travel there with the rank of major. At Murmansk he would join 150 Canadian soldiers trained in Arctic survival. As far as the war effort was concerned, his time, it appeared, had come.

Shackleton's commanding officer in Russia was General Charles Maynard. Maynard was less than impressed by what he had heard of Shackleton before his arrival. He had expected a man who was difficult, if not impossible, to get on with. Once he got to know Shackleton his impression changed: 'From the moment of his arrival to the time of his departure ... he gave me of his very best, and his loyalty from start to finish was absolute. He fitted at once into the niche awaiting him.'

Reunited with Hussey, Macklin, Worsley and Stenhouse, Shackleton was, suddenly, optimistic again. Ill health, disappointment, financial worries were all put aside as adventure took centre stage.

With no particular task that he could call his own, he took charge of organizing the camp and was popular with most of the men – officers and rank and file soldiers. He looked after clothing, rations and equipment but he never saw action.

On 17 May 1918 he wrote one of his affectionate letters home, to Cecily at school at Rodean: 'Do you think they would take me as a janitor at Rodean or could I come as a Professor of Ice and Snow? Your tottering aged Daddy Ernest Shackleton.' And, on 26 October, from Syrea: 'I hope girlie that you are putting in some good work at school this term ... Work and punctuality and being tidy are three good things and after a little attention all this comes naturally.'

In November the war proper ended and a month later he returned to London with Maynard, to try to get further supplies for the men in Russia. While in England he spent a short time with his family but on Christmas Day he and Maynard set sail again.

In January the Murmansk force was mustered to travel to Archangel, a distance of 150 miles, to fight the Bolsheviks. Shackleton was suddenly busy arranging provisions, packing sledges and giving advice, but to his disappointment, he was not included in the actual party.

The reality was brought home to him. He might play at soldiering but he was not regarded as a soldier. They might use his talents but they would never see him as an equal on the battlefield. The adventure of war, which was to have followed the great adventure in Antarctica, was proving to be nothing more than a peripheral service to those in the thick of the action.

At times he was saddened by this, at other times angered, feeling the gifts he possessed were subordinated by those who knew less about the business of survival in an Arctic landscape than he did.

While anger had to be curtailed in camp, it found expression in his letters: 'Sometimes I … feel … part of my youth is slipping away from me and that nothing matters,' he wrote to Emily. 'I want to upset everybody's calm and peace of mind when I meet calm and contented people. I feel I am no use to anyone unless I am outfacing the storm.'

The war ended without his seeing any action. In February he resigned his position in the army but he believed his financial security might still lie in north Russia. He planned to use the destitution of the population as a foundation from which they, he and the British government might benefit. He would establish a company, raise capital and send supplies of clothing and other essentials to the impoverished people of the area. In return, the North Russian government would give him a 99-year lease on sections of Murmansk, which would then be developed for British interests. Furthermore, his company would be given exploration rights for minerals and the right to use White Sea ports for trading. Everybody would prosper, everybody would be happy.

Finance was the key to the plan, as it was to most things in Shackleton's life. He was convinced that the required money, somewhere in the region of £2,000,000, could be raised without difficulty; the opportunities were clear to him and would, he assumed, be so to potential investors. He met the Assistant Governor-General of the area and the plan

Inscriptions at front of South*: EHS, F. Wild, F. Worsley, J.R. Stenhouse (1887–1941) was Chief Officer of the Aurora 1914–1915. He served with distinction in both wars. Leonard Hussey, who provided cheerful music with his banjo on the* Endurance *and the* Quest, *accompanied Shackleton's body after his death to Montevideo and then back to Grytviken for the burial. James Archibald McIlroy was surgeon on the* Endurance *and later on the* Quest. *His parents were from Greencastle, County Antrim, and they moved to Birmingham. Later James worked as a ship's doctor; he had a colourful love life but died a bachelor.*

appeared to be making headway. Returning to England in March, he poured his energies into the enterprise but North Russia was to fall to the Revolutionaries before anything came of the great design.

While the North Russian possibilities were being explored, he needed to continue to make a living. During the summer of 1919 he returned to the dreaded lecture circuit. Though thoroughly sick of lecturing, it served the dual purpose of raising money and keeping him away from home.

In November *South*, his account of the trans-Antarctic expedition, was published and the response was extremely positive and sales good. A claim, however, from the executors of one of his benefactors meant that the money coming from the sales was diverted to the benefactor's estate, and Shackleton never saw a penny of the profits.

Some money did come from the sales of rights to the film he had made of the Antarctic expedition but again this was confused by his allocating some of these rights to Ernest Joyce and then finding himself at loggerheads with Joyce about what exactly had been agreed.

In December he began a series of lectures and slide-shows at the Philharmonic Hall in Portland Street, London. The series was to run for five months with two lectures a day, accompanied by the showing of the film. Attendance was mediocre but the series made him a living. One can only imagine the absolute tedium of re-telling the same stories over and over, often to a half-empty house.

Yet, this was to be the spur that saw him turn his attention to a grander escape from rows of peering faces. He would return to being an explorer and leave behind the second-hand life of talking about it.

His newest plan was to move north, to explore the unexplored Beaufort Sea and, possibly, to try for the North Pole. Alexander Macklin became his confidant. In February 1920 he wrote to the Royal Geographical Society and they approved the idea but suggested he approach the Canadian government. By the time he had finished his lecture series in May he'd been in touch with the Canadians and they, too, were supportive. Both *The Times* and the *Daily Mail* offered to help with pre- and post-expedition publicity and by the summer's end Shackleton was busy plotting and planning. He drew up a prospectus to raise interest in, and money for, his latest scheme.

If the lecture series in the Philharmonic had seemed like an endless echo to Shackleton, his plans for the Arctic trip must have sounded similar to those who knew him. He was counting on the support of a few wealthy backers, rather than trying to draw small amounts from a wide number of people. He contacted the Admiralty in the hope that they would fit out the expedition vessel, and hoped the British government would assist with funding. And *The Times* carried the public announcement of Shackleton's latest plan of adventure.

The dawn of 1921 brought a rush of activity. In January he was in Norway looking at a whaling ship, the *Foca I*. In February the details of the expedition were published, outlining plans to take twelve men and to collect 150 huskies at Hudson Bay and then to travel on, via Baffin Bay, into Lancaster Sound and so to the Beaufort Sea.

At the end of February he went to Canada and received the blessing of the Canadian government. A month later his plans had altered slightly and he informed Hugh Robert Mill that he was going to take fifteen men in total on the trip. By then he had renamed the ship the *Quest* and was preparing for a second visit to Canada in April. Now there was no time for monotony, no doubts about age and stimulation. He might not be going south again but he was going.

Shackleton arrived back in England from Canada on 19 May and nine days later Macklin set off for Canada to collect the dogs. Just over three weeks on Macklin found himself in Winnipeg with a new Canadian government and a shift in policy on the question of expeditions. Money was tight in Canada and none would be wasted on fripperies like Arctic exploration.

Within days Macklin received a wire from Shackleton, telling him to return home and informing him that the *Quest* would 'carry out Antarctic coast survey and Southern islands exploration'. He had decided that an expedition would go ahead – the destination was no longer the important part. The ship had been bought, much of the money was in, the men were standing by. He would once more head south.

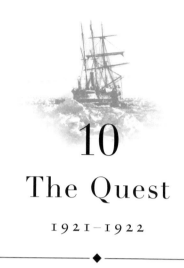

10

The Quest

1921–1922

◆

The *Quest* expedition was Shackleton's last great throw of the dice. Aged forty-seven, he was still a reasonably young man but his energy was not what it had been. In his enthusiasm to ensure it went ahead, he attempted to interest as many people in as wide a prospectus as could be managed.

For the economists among his audience he maintained there was money to be made in the sub-Antarctic from exploiting everything from coal, oil, phosphate and nickel deposits to guano, pearl fishing, whaling and sealing.

For the geographers there was the possibility of finding lost islands, improving charts and mapping 2000 miles of the coast of Enderby Land.

For marine biologists there was the promise of what dredging work might reveal.

For meteorologists there was the prospect of finding good sites for wireless and meteorology stations.

And, for the emerging Air Ministry there was the undertaking to look for suitable airfield locations.

In the matter of finance, Shackleton was, for once, blessed. His old school friend John Quiller Rowett, who had shared his walks home from school in Dulwich and who had gone on to make a fortune in the rum business, undertook to pay whatever Shackleton hadn't managed to raise towards the Antarctic expedition. This was a gesture of extraordinary

Shackleton, Rowett and Wild in 1921. John Quiller Rowett (1876-1924), an old Dulwich College friend, was the main backer of the Shackleton-Rowett expedition in the Quest *having made money supplying rum to the Royal Navy.*

generosity and, although Shackleton offered to repay the money from whatever books, lectures and films that followed the *Quest* expedition, Rowett must have known the money might never materialize. He agreed that Shackleton should be allowed to go ahead on his own terms. Those, as Shackleton had outlined, were that he would 'have an absolute veto on everything ... I am opposed as a matter of principle root and branch, with the interference of Committees.'

While the *Quest* was a smaller ship than the *Endurance*, too small in the view of Hugh Robert Mill, Shackleton got to work on fitting her out with all the modern paraphernalia he could muster. This aspect of the expedition caught the attention of the press and the public, and a stream of stories appeared in newspapers outlining the range of gadgets on board the ship. Everything, from the electrically heated crow's nest to the most up to date wireless set to the electric Odograph which would record the *Quest's* course and speeds, became the focus of the reporters' attention. Mill thought Shackleton was attempting too much in a ship that, while equipped with modern conveniences, was ill suited to the difficult work that lay ahead.

Some geographers were resistant to the use of modern equipment in expedition work, particularly where its use drew public attention. Sir Clements Markham had believed that anything that caught the imagination of the masses must be suspect.

But for that very public, of which the scientists and geographers were so suspicious, Shackleton was a light in the darkness that followed the Great War. So many hopes had died and been buried in the battlefields of Europe that it seemed there might never be another dream to displace the nightmare of loss and death. And now here was the man the people loved undertaking another adventure, pursuing his dream with such conviction that people couldn't but believe he would succeed.

Shackleton thrived on the image of himself as the explorer. He told the *Daily Graphic*: 'I go exploring because I like it and because it's my job … So I return to the wild again and again until, I suppose, in the end the wild will win.'

Like an old cricket team, they reassembled for another tilt at a prize that had long eluded them, Shackleton naming the names: Worsley as captain; Wild and McIlroy appearing back from Africa in answer to the call; James Dell, who had missed the *Endurance* expedition through illness, and D.G. Jeffrey, who'd missed it because of the war, were there.

Charles Green, the cook who'd kept body and soul together on the *Endurance*, was back in the galley, and Alfred Kerr, another *Endurance* man, was signed as second engineer. Leonard Hussey, now qualified as a doctor, was on board, as was Alexander Macklin. James Dell and Thomas McLeod made up the eleventh and twelfth men of the old boys' network. Shackleton was at the helm of a crew he knew and trusted, and who knew and trusted him.

And there were new men, too. Hubert Wilkins, who had first met Shackleton in 1912, was taken as a biologist, and Roderick Carr, who had made his acquaintance in Russia, was entrusted with responsibility for flying the plane which Shackleton planned to take. Both

Wilkins, who had an interest in aircraft, and Carr worked on the design of the 80-horse-power monoplane which was to be another of the innovations that would make this expedition so unique.

There was another radical difference that raised hackles on many fronts. Emily Shackleton had become involved in the Girl Guide movement and, when the *Daily Mail* proposed offering a place on the *Quest* to a Boy Scout, she wholeheartedly endorsed the idea.

The newspaper's advertisement drew almost 1700 applications and these were whittled down to a manageable ten, who were then interviewed on 18 August 1921 by Shackleton himself. The telegrams sent out the following day to the families of the unsuccessful applicants told the whole story. 'Shackleton selecting Marr and Mooney, but wanted to take the lot.' Unable to choose between Norman Mooney and James Marr, he opted to take both.

This publicity stunt drew criticism from those who already thought the serious scientific nature of the *Quest* expedition was being overshadowed by an insatiable desire for publicity.

Choosing two young men who had no experience of life at sea, no particular gifts to bring to the expedition and were, simply, a source of newspaper columns, before the ship set sail, was definitely at odds with Shackleton's care in surrounding himself with tried and trusted comrades. As it happened, by the time the *Quest* reached Madeira, Mooney had fallen so ill with seasickness that Shackleton decided he was unfit to continue his adventure and should return home.

As with previous expeditions, the ship was on view to the public as a fund-raiser for charity. Given the wealth of gadgetry on board and the pressure to get her fitted in time, however, the public had to content themselves with viewing the *Quest* from the quayside.

Shackleton's relationship with the Admiralty continued to be patchy. They offered him assistance in installing the radio on the *Quest* and made maps available. But this was done only after he had paid just over £200 for borrowed instruments, which had gone down on the *Endurance*.

Preceding the *Quest's* departure, finances were in place, the public was behind Shackleton, even the Admiralty and the Royal Geographical Society had rowed in, granted without any great enthusiasm and with qualms about the company Shackleton was keeping.

Yet the expedition lacked focus, not just in the diversity of its objectives but in Shackleton's approach. He was looking forward to the adventure but was also unwell, suffering from back, shoulder and chest pains, and tiredness. Shortly before they sailed, Hussey insisted on taking him to see a specialist at King's Hospital in London about constant pains in his feet. The specialist diagnosed nothing more serious than flat feet and suggested that Shackleton wear supports in his boots. Otherwise, he was given a clean bill of health.

Emily, noting that he was not in particularly good shape and worried by his chronic tiredness also insisted he see a specialist but, according to McIlroy, Shackleton 'examined the specialist instead of the specialist examining him' and put his lack of energy down to middle age.

Many things less serious than a life-threatening illness could have explained the aches and pains. He was not as fit as he had been and he was a heavy smoker. The years since his last expedition saw him drinking more than he ought and taking less exercise than he might. He lived under constant stress – both personally and financially, in his marriage and the promises of repayment from unwritten books, unmade films and undelivered lectures.

EHS, his wife Emily and their children, Cecily, Raymond and Eddie, aboard the Quest 15 August 1921; that summer he was based with his family at 14 Milnthorpe Road, Eastbourne, Sussex.

Of course, there were other factors which wore Shackleton down. His times in the Antarctic had been demanding, physically and mentally. The *Endurance* trip took a huge amount out of him and the constant sniping which followed had eaten into his confidence. The *Quest* expedition, in spite of all the great ambitions riding on it, might be viewed as aimless, and Shackleton knew this. It had none of the driving focus of its predecessors. It could be seen as a simple escape from England and a promise of almost inevitable disappointment.

There were no circumstances in which all its ambitions could be met, rather the expedition was an end in itself, a last voyage to be followed by the inevitable anticlimax of real life.

So often, Shackleton had set off with his beloved Browning's lines in his head, 'when the fight begins within himself, a man's worth something'. But this time there was little of that fight in his heart.

Yet, as the day of departure grew closer, something of the old adventurer returned to haunt the body of the man and he was, if only briefly, the shining giant of England. *The Times* wrote of his spirit turning 'old men into wistful youths' and, it continued 'There is nothing for us to do but wish him good luck.'

EHS bids farewell – looking frail with cigarette in hand, saying goodbye for the last time.

On 18 September the *Quest* left London for Plymouth. This time there was no war to distract from the farewell and the quays were thronged with crowds wishing the ship and her crew

Quest in the Pool of London, summer 1921. An uncomfortable mover on the sea, this small Norwegian sealer, built in 1917, was finally claimed by the ice north of Newfoundland in 1962.

bon voyage. Shackleton rejoined the ship in Plymouth and, following a farewell dinner hosted by Rowett, the *Quest* set sail on 24 September. Shackleton wrote: '... shore and sea are still and in the calm lazy gathering dusk on a glassy sea we move on the long Quest. Providence is with us even now ... I turn from the glooming mystic immensity of the sea and looking at the decks of the *Quest* am roused from dreams of what may be in the future to the needs of the moment.'

What he didn't record was an observation made to the Harbourmaster in Portsmouth. As they passed a buoy, with its slowly tolling bell, McIlroy overheard Shackleton say: 'That's my death knell.'

Whatever about the troubles that lay ahead, those first days at sea were a time of tranquillity and relaxation after the manic preparations of previous months. Three days into the voyage he noted in his diary that he had 'stopped the wireless operator from taking in the news last night it is of no importance to us now in a little world of our own'.

These moments of serenity, however, proved illusory. Not only was the *Quest* small and heavily laden, but she was much slower than Shackleton had expected. Eight knots per hour had been promised but, even in calm conditions, the little ship was finding it difficult to maintain five and a half. Within five days of leaving Portsmouth Shackleton realized he would have to alter his plans, as his diary entry of 28 September records:

'*[The Quest] must be treated as a five knot vessel ... I am tied to time for the ice ... I can see that our decks need to be absolutely clear when we are in the roaring forties. Her foremast also gives me anxiety ... The main thing is that I may have to curtail our island programme in order to get to the Cape in time ... Everyone is cheerful which is a blessing all singing and enjoying themselves though pretty well wet: several are a bit sick ... These are just random thoughts: but borne in on one as it all being so different from the other strain of preparation: it is a blessing that this time I have not the financial worry or strain.*'

186

EHS and Worsley, one of the last photographs of them together. The New Zealander Frank Worsley (1872-1943) was a superb navigator and seaman who made the boat journey from Elephant Island to South Georgia possible.

After encountering stormy weather in the Bay of Biscay, the *Quest* developed a knock in the engine. There was nothing for it but to put into port in Lisbon. Although the crew could ill afford this loss of time and the added expense, there was no alternative, the work had to be done and so, on 2 October the ship berthed and work began on her engines.

A week later she was making for Madeira where she docked 16 October. Having come through particularly bad storms, Shackleton decided that the photographer Bee Mason and the scout Mooney, who'd shown little sign of recovery from severe seasickness, should return home. Nor was this loss of two crewmen the greatest of the problems blown in on the gales. The rigging of the ship had been strained and constant buffeting had bent the crankshaft. Writing from Madeira, Shackleton recounted his problems to Emily and continued: 'This is a lonely life after all … I miss you … and I love you.'

187

At St Vincent, in the Cape Verde Islands, Gerald Lysaght left the *Quest*, as planned, to return to England, and Shackleton wrote to Emily telling her he felt ill but reassuring her that in a couple of days he'd be back to his old self.

The next leg of the expedition ran more smoothly, but Shackleton decided to dock in Rio de Janeiro for a full overhaul, to find a remedy for the recurring engine problems.

The Atlantic crossing was made in calm hot weather, to the delight of all but the stokers. As she steamed, Shackleton organized the repainting of the ship – changing the colours from yellow and white to black and grey.

On 22 November the *Quest* arrived in Rio and there she was to stay for almost four weeks. The work she underwent was major. The engines were stripped and repaired. The rigging was fixed and extensions were built to the deck-house.

The crew went in various directions, some remaining in Rio, some journeying farther afield. Wilkins and Douglas travelled ahead by steamer to do research work on South Georgia until the *Quest* called to collect them.

Captain Sharpus, who worked in Wilson's shipyard where the *Quest* had gone for repairs, recalled the stress the ship was causing Shackleton. 'Everything in the engine room of that ship seemed to be wrong ... I knew he was worried almost to death. I dreaded him meeting ... the ship's engineer or ... our engineer ... for fear they'd tell him some new trouble. I could see by his face it hurt him so. All his hopes and ambitions seemed centred in that little ship, and she seemed to let him down so much that I got to hate the damned boat.'

Shackleton's days were spent at the shipyard 'on an island baking hot with mosquitoes and clanging hammers all day', and many of his nights in Rio were occupied by 'some long drawn out function' and 'all the time I am mad to get away'.

The added delay led Shackleton to the decision not to visit Cape Town, even though some of his equipment, including essential parts for the aeroplane, had been sent there for collection. He had been told the *Quest*'s engines were not up to heavy work in the ice and the choices were stark. Go south as soon as possible and do as much as could be done as quickly as possible, or abandon the expedition.

By now, much of the *Quest*'s planned itinerary had been changed and it was decided she would sail south with three new crewmen – Young, Argles and Naisbitt, a South African, a Canadian and an Englishman. Naisbitt recalled his interview with Shackleton in Rio. He had arrived wearing a suit and a hat and Shackleton asked 'if I had ever done a day's work in my life. I said I had served in the Navy four years and that I was fond of sport ... He asked if I realized I might have to carry meals from the galley to the forward mess, the little ship rolling and pitching in heavy seas and the decks awash most of the time. I told him I was sure I could do the job. He asked me

Rio de Janiero November-December 1921, probably the last photograph of Shackleton on land. He never liked the heat, and the stress was increased by troubles with the ship's engines and his own heart.

what I was doing in Rio and I told him. Then he seemed to hesitate and endeavoured to discourage me: thinking no doubt I was throwing away my commercial career but he saw I was keen.'

Writing from Rio, Shackleton admitted the state of his mental health to Emily:

'I have been in a whirl and strain ever since we came in: Everything seemed to go wrong twice the engines had to be altered ... altogether it has been hell. Now it is 110 degrees in the shade ... I only just write this to say that you must not worry about me and that my health is really all right ... I am going to take no risks in the ice so don't worry ... I am doing my best.'

There was something particularly forlorn in that last phrase. Shackleton had never been one to talk of doing his best, rather he had been the one who got things done in spite of everything. His P.S. was to prove closer to the truth: 'Darling I am a little tired but all right you seem always young.'

It was 16 December.

The following evening Shackleton and Captain Sharpus were working on accounts on board the *Quest*. Most of the men were ashore, enjoying a final evening of freedom before their departure the following day. When a boat came to take Sharpus back to shore, Shackleton, who had been feeling unwell, asked if he might accompany him and get some air. He spent the night on land and the following day, when Macklin came to check on him, he claimed to have recovered from what was simply a fainting spell due to the hot weather. He refused to undergo any medical examination. Sharpus, however, maintained that Shackleton had suffered a heart attack and both doctors, Macklin and McIlroy, set sail on 18 December, uncertain about the true state of their leader's health. Shackleton warned them not to talk about his illness and insisted that he was completely better. Both men advised him to rest and, surprisingly, he didn't argue.

Macklin noted in his diary that Shackleton was subdued and seemed to want to talk more than he had formerly done, yet he was uncertain about what he would do when the *Quest* got south. Macklin wrote, 'I do not quite understand his enigmatical attitude – I wonder what we really shall do.'

To see Shackleton uncertain about where the *Quest* would go and how she would spend the winter and what exactly the expedition would achieve was alarming for Macklin and those who had previously travelled with him. Something was not right with the Boss, but he dismissed the concerns of those about him.

Another worrying trait was Shackleton's recent practice of opening a bottle of champagne each morning, a startling change for a man who had frowned on the use of alcohol on board ship, other than on festive occasions.

To reduce the Boss's workload, Macklin suggested that responsibility for the running of the ship might, to some extent, be delegated to Worsley and Wild – both experienced men. Shackleton listened without arguing, but continued his own workload.

Everything about the expedition – the immensity of the undertaking, Shackleton's attempt to cover as many angles as possible, the publicity of taking the two boy scouts on board, even the decision to go south when the Canadian Arctic Expedition was cancelled – spoke of desperation.

A fine, bright, calm Christmas Eve gave way to a Christmas Day that saw a full force gale pummelling the ship. Christmas dinner was cancelled and Green supplied the men with sandwiches and cocoa. The wind and rain continued through the night into the following day, and the calmer weather, when it came, brought news that one of the fresh water tanks had leaked and was dry. Another raging storm blew up on 27 December. Shackleton had already been on watch or on call through the Christmas Day gale and now continued on the bridge. His own cabin had been flooded and what sleep he took was taken in snatches in the wardroom. The storm, he said, was the worst he had ever endured and, by the time it abated on the 28th he and everyone on board was drained. But the *Quest* had one final trick to play.

No sooner had the weather improved than Kerr, the Second Engineer, discovered a leak in the ship's furnace. At best it meant a reduction in speed until they reached South Georgia. At worst it might mean the end of the expedition. To the exhausted Shackleton it was another kick when his spirit was already down.

Christopher Naisbitt was to witness a side of Shackleton that was rarely seen. 'When the Boss is annoyed about something it seems to upset him altogether – nothing is right. At mealtimes there is something to complain about – the plates have not been warmed for the hot dishes – his macaroni cheese is not sufficiently crisp – or something else is wrong. Capt. Hussey seems to be a very useful man in this direction … he generally administers the right dope for a boisterous Irish spirit and after a while you find Dr Jekyll climbing out of Mr Hyde.'

Shackleton was suffering from constant back and face pains, and the heavy weather through which the ship was passing meant there was no time to sleep properly.

On 1 January 1922, as the weather at last improved, he returned to his diary, which had been ignored during the gales: 'The year has begun kindly for us: it is curious how a certain date becomes a factor and milestone in ones life: Christmas Day in the raging gale seemed out of place I dared not hope that today would be as it was: Anxiety has been probing deeply into me: for until the very end of the year things have gone awry …"There are two points in the adventures of the diver" one when a beggar, he prepares to plunge one when a prince he rises with his pearl.'

He wasn't the only anxious one. Macklin and McIlroy were watching the Boss carefully. Both knew his physical problems, and both knew he wasn't taking their advice.

For Shackleton, this return to the southern ocean cut through the freezing wastes of memory. On 2 January he spotted an iceberg and wrote about 'the years that have gone since in the pride of young manhood I first went forth to the fight I grow old and tired but must always lead'.

The last known photograph of Shackleton, chatting with his old friend the Yorkshireman Frank Wild, who travelled on four expeditions to the Antarctic. Wild's leadership of the remaining party on Elephant Island in 1916 was exceptional; very much Shackleton's other self. He mixed with and earned the respect of all sorts of people. Died in South Africa 1939 in miserable circumstances.

There is sense of enormus foreboding and heavy-heartedness in this and later diary entries, as though the cold bright waters and rising icebergs were no longer sufficient to lighten the closing shadows.

Continuing fine weather and then the sighting of South Georgia on 4 January saw Shackleton's pessimism lift somewhat and he, Wild and Worsley surveyed the outline of their old haunts. As the day wore on Shackleton took the *Quest* into Grytviken harbour and anchored her where the *Endurance* had once dropped anchor. Later he went ashore and revisited the scenes of his former adventure, spending time with the station manager, Jacobsen, and rambling around the familiar places before returning to the ship and promising that, on the morrow, the crew would celebrate the Christmas Day they had missed in the storm.

That night Shackleton played a few hands of cards with McIlroy before telling the doctor he was tired and going to his cabin. Once there, he wrote in his diary: '… after 16 days of turmoil and anxiety: on a peaceful sunshiny day we came to anchor in Gryviken [sic]. How

familiar the coast seemed as we passed down … Now we must speed all we can but the
prospect is not too bright for labour is scarce. The old smell of dead whale permeates everything: It is a strange and curious place. Douglas and Wilkins are at different ends of the
island. A wonderful evening. "In the darkening twilight I saw a lone star hover, gem like
above the bay."'

The shadow was about to envelop him.

Just after two o'clock on the morning of 5 January, Macklin answered a whistle call
from Shackleton's cabin. He spoke with the Boss and then went back to his watch. A short
time afterwards the whistle sounded again and Macklin returned to the cabin. In his diary
he recorded the remaining events of those early hours:

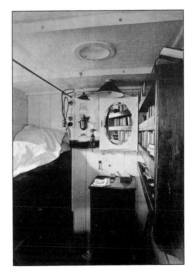

EHS death cabin
on the Quest.
Later occupied
by Wild.

'He told me that he was suffering from pains in the
back & bad facial neuralgia. He wished for some drug
that would produce immediate relief. He said he had
taken 3 tablets of aspirin & that they had done him no
good. I noticed he was covered in only one blanket &
as the night was cold I said "You should be more
warmly covered. I will get you my blanket" which I
did & tucked it all around him. He was impatient
however for some drug to immediately relieve him of
pain & to give him sleep. I left him & went to the
medicine cupboard & got 10 minims of Chlorodyne,
which I gave him in water. He did not take it at once
but said "put it down there while I talk to you". He
then said I do not believe that aspirin is any good it
takes too long to act, will that stuff of yours act
quickly." I told him "yes". He asked "what is the cause of this trouble of mine" & I told
him, as I had told him many times before, that he had been overdoing things, & that it was
no good expecting any single dose of medicine to put him right, but that it was much more
important to try & lead a more regular life, get sleep regularly, have a good daily motion
of the bowels & have a regular simple diet. He replied "You're always wanting me to give

193

up things, what is it I ought to give up". I replied "chiefly alcohol Boss I don't think it agrees with you". He then said "I can feel the pain coming again give me the medicine quickly". He swallowed it but immediately had a very severe paroxysm during which he died. I stopped by him till I saw that all was hopeless & then went to McIlroy for it flashed through my mind that his death would cause a sensation & that there might be an inquiry & said "Mick come at once and see the Boss he is dying." He came but on entering the room said as soon as he saw him "Yes! He's gone". Naturally it staggered us & for a few moments we said & did nothing. Then we woke up Wild & told him, & later Worsley. On my way to McIlroy I also woke Hussey & told him to get a hypodermic injection of ether ready at once but did not give it as it would have been quite useless. Death is a terrible thing & I can never get used to it, but this was much more so, as can easily be understood. The cause of death is, I feel perfectly sure, angina pectoris. I laid him out & fixed things up, turned out the lamp, which was burning, & shut the door.'

It wasn't until breakfast time that the crew was called together by Wild. Some of them thought the expedition was being abandoned due to lack of money. When they had gathered, Wild spoke. 'Boys,' he said, 'I've got some sad news for you. The Boss died suddenly at three o'clock this morning. The expedition will carry on.'

   Later in the morning, Macklin, McIlroy and Wild went ashore to notify the local magistrate of Shackleton's death and to arrange for a death certificate. Even then nothing went

Grytviken and Quest *in King Edward Cove, South Georgia. Shackleton's final anchorage.*

smoothly. As there was no wireless on South Georgia and the set on the *Quest* was not functioning, Wild was delegated to go to Leith where the *Albuera* was anchored, and have her send out the news as soon as she sailed within range of a wireless station. This was to be only the first of many decisions and changes of mind that would follow in the wake of his death.

Shackleton's body was sewn into canvas and taken to the hospital in Grytviken where, on 7 January, his remains were injected with formalin and Hussey arranged for the body to be carried by steamer to Montevideo and thence to England. He would accompany the remains while the rest of the crew went on with the expedition, under Wild's command, something they knew Shackleton would have wanted.

On 19 January the body left South Georgia aboard the *Professor Gruvel,* arriving in Montevideo ten days later. As ever, the Uruguayans were fulsome in their honouring of Shackleton. They had fêted him in life and so they showed their respect for him in death.

EHS's coffin, nurses and Hussey (centre left), in the Military Hospital, Montevideo, where Shackleton's body lay for two weeks until the memorial service. The nurses kept fresh red and white roses from the hospital garden on his coffin.

Crew of the Quest building a memorial cairn on King Edward Point after returning to Grytviken in April 1922.

His coffin was greeted by one hundred cadets and taken, draped in the Union Jack, to the military hospital. There, a guard of honour stood by it day and night and fresh roses were placed on it daily by the hospital staff.

As soon as the news of her husband's death, and the planned return of his body reached Emily, she decided that the appropriate place for his burial was the place where he had died, the island that had been so important to him and that had now claimed him. Recognizing better than most, that south was where Shackleton's soul was drawn, she had no doubt that south was where his body belonged and she asked the Uruguayan authorities to return her husband's body for burial to South Georgia.

Once the request reached Uruguay, the President, Baltasar Brum, ordered full military honours for the re-embarkation of the coffin. Writing of Shackleton, he referred to his 'magnificent … humanity … in an age of warlike heroism he was the hero, calm and strong, who left behind him neither death nor grief'.

On St Valentine's day Shackleton's remains were brought to the Holy Trinity Church and on 15 February the president, ministers of the government and foreign dignitaries attended a memorial service. After the service, Shackleton's coffin was placed on a gun carriage and a salute fired.

On the quays, the coffin was formally handed over to the British *chargé d'affaires*, Edward Hope Vere, and taken on board the British streamer *Woodville*. The following morning a Uruguayan cruiser, the *Uruguay*, accompanied the steamer to the limit of the country's territorial waters where another gun salute saw her on her way. On 27 February Shackleton's body arrived back on South Georgia in a blizzard.

On 5 March a service was held in the Lutheran church in Grytviken, led by a Mr Binnie, the local English magistrate. The church was crowded, as the church on Uruguay had been, but this time the congregation was made up of sailors, station workers, whaling men and local people. Afterwards Shackleton's coffin was carried across the rough South Georgian ground and laid to rest at last.

There were wreaths from the British and Uruguayan governments and one from the people of South Georgia made by a Mrs Aarberg, the only woman on the island. The crew of the *Quest,* then steaming south through the ice, was represented by Leonard Hussey. A plain wooden cross stood above the grave. Its simplicity, the final homecoming of the sailor from the sea, was more eloquent than the accolades and editorials that followed his death.

On 6 April, a month after Shackleton's burial, the *Quest* returned to South Georgia and his comrades built a stone cairn on a site overlooking the harbour in Grytviken. Macklin wrote in his diary: 'Wild took the cross which Dell had made & which Kerr and Smith had secured into a drum, & erected it in the cairn. The cairn with the cross forms a conspicuous mark. I think this is as "the Boss" would have had it himself, standing lonely in an island far from civilisation, surrounded by stormy tempestuous seas, & in the vicinity of one of his greatest exploits. It is likely to be seen by few, but the few who see it are men who themselves lead hard lives, & who are able to appreciate better than those at home, the work which he accomplished.'

11

The Legend

◆

Shackleton's death, a quiet passing that had none of the elements of the heroic posthumously foisted on Scott's memory, was regretted and forgotten beyond the circle of his family and friends. In death, as in life, he was an outsider. Had his body been brought back to England there would, doubtless, have been an enormous and communal outpouring of grief, but that too is a transient thing. The public, who had loved him and made him its own, mourned his passing. For a time, some of Browning's words from 'The Lost Leader' were particularly apposite:

> *'We that had loved him so, followed him, honoured him,*
> *Lived in his mild and magnificent eye,*
> *Learned his great language, caught his clear accents,*
> *Made him our pattern to live and to die.'*

But the 1920s were a difficult time for the working people of England, those very people who had taken Shackleton to their hearts. Post-war England was no longer filled with the optimism that had taken the country into a world war, and the smell of victory was little different from the smell of defeat. Most families carried with them the grief for lost sons and fathers, brothers and husbands, and the struggle for survival left little time or energy for remembering dead champions.

Unveiling of rugged granite headstone by Governor of the Falklands, Arnold Hodson, 25 February 1928. Carved by Stewart McGlashen, Edinburgh, the inscription reads, 'I hold that a man should strive to the uttermost for his life's set prize', adapted from a poem by Robert Browning, 'The Statue and the Bust', which correctly reads: 'Let a man contend to the uttermost for his life's set prize, be that what it will.'

In Ireland, newly independent but in the throes of a civil war, Shackleton was never likely to be viewed heroically. Despite his triumphant return as a lecturer in the previous decade and his roots by birth, childhood and family history in the country, there was little empathy in the new state with a man seen as British, a man who had carried the Union Jack to Antarctica.

In Britain, where his memory might have been cherished, his standing in death as in life was beyond the pale. He had never played the establishment game and while individual geographers admired his spirit, the Royal Geographical Society already had one dead hero on its hands and an Englishman at that.

Shackleton's true home was on that no man's land of ice and snow where nationality meant nothing and comradeship meant everything. His final resting-place, among the whalers and sailors of northern Europe, displaced men whose ambitions had been washed up on the bleak shores of South Georgia, was chillingly appropriate.

After the rush to praise, a public silence descended. Behind the scenes, however, a committee was established to gather funds for Emily and the children and for Shackleton's mother and two of his sisters, whom he had been supporting at the time of his death.

Hugh Robert Mill, one of Shackleton's closest friends and greatest admirers, set to work on a biography. He was well placed to write the book, knowing Shackleton and being one of his confidantes and having Emily's assistance in preparing the work. He, also, brought a sense of objectivity in the assessment of Shackleton's life.

Following the publication of Mill's book, *The Life of Sir Ernest Shackleton*, in April 1923, there were other memorials. A headstone was erected in South Georgia in 1928. In 1932 a statue was unveiled by the Marquis of Zetland, but gradually the memory of Shackleton faded from the public consciousness.

Shackleton's statue by Charles Jagger, unveiled in January 1932. Originally designed for a plinth, it was placed in a niche in the buildings of the Royal Geographical Society at a busy junction of Exhibition Road and Kensington Gore, London.

At the same time, the deification of Scott continued. He was the man whose heroism still overshadowed Shackleton's. Scott grew comfortably into the role of martyr. Shackleton was too intuitive and too much an individual to fit the image demanded by the establishment.

While one of his great strengths was the technical planning of supplies for expeditions, when it came to decision-making on the ground, Shackleton's intuition was the basis for almost everything. And, once that intuition had been followed, responsibility and loyalty were expected and given as an integral part of the comradeship he developed with his crew. Recognizing their enthusiasm and affection, Shackleton would lead only to places from which he felt he could safely return. His men were not expendable. Much has been made of the poetic side of Shackleton's nature and it is true that he saw himself literally and metaphorically in the role of poet adventurer. He never allowed his poetic vision to cloud his common sense, however, and in that regard he was much less limited in his vision than Scott.

Leonard Hussey was to write of him: 'He would often say to me when some particularly brave or daring act was brought to his notice, " … the quality that I look for most is optimism: especially optimism in the face of reverses and apparent defeat. Optimism is true moral courage." '

Nor was Shackleton some kind of early twentieth-century saint. He was fiercely independent but he never shirked responsibility for his decisions. His comrades were well aware of his fallibility and he never sought to disguise it.

Nowhere was this aspect of the man more evident than in his personal life, whose complexity makes him even more intriguing. It was this complexity as much as anything that allowed Emily to live with his foibles and without his practical support. She recognized that, most of the time, he gave what he could.

As soon as Emily was his, her love became secondary to his ambition. He would say that he wished to keep her in the style she deserved but there was never a time when he allowed shortage of money to stop his travelling. Indeed, as the years went by, he would grow to depend on her for his financial security.

The onset of middle age and the certainty of his decreasing physical strength were painful propositions for Shackleton. Life was running ahead of him and he could no longer keep pace with it. For a man whose time had been spent in the pursuit of physical fulfilment, this was alarming. The older he grew, the more he fought against age.

The adoration of women was one of the temporary stays against decay. He was not alone in his inability to love only one woman but that inability did nothing to assuage his constant feelings of deep guilt. He believed that love, like financial security, would always be found somewhere else.

Shackleton's death and his subsequent demotion to supporting Scott meant that much of the complexity of his personality and life was forgotten. Not until the 1950s, and the appearance of Margery and James Fisher's book, *Shackleton*, in 1957, and Alfred Lansing's *Endurance* in 1959, did the revival of interest in the explorer begin.

Both Roland Huntford's *Shackleton*, published in 1985, and Caroline Alexander's *The Endurance. Shackleton's Legendary Antarctic Expedition*, which appeared in 1999, added greatly to the understanding and rehabilitation of the man.

Ironically, at a time when Scott's star appears to be fading, Shackleton's is brighter than ever. He is the one most often chosen by people as the person they would like to have travelled with to the Antarctic. Shackleton has recently been taken up as an icon by management firms who regularly refer to him as the perfect example of the ideal manager, the man who got all his crew back safely from each of his expeditions. Shackleton hated the notion of management by numbers. This transformation into some kind of super man-manager does him an enormous disservice. Worst of all, it ignores his troubled heart. Shackleton was not a type, he was a man, embued with bravery but flawed.

Failure, as much as anything, made him the man he was. He saw little that was glorious in his decision to abandon an expedition that had all but reached the Pole or in the struggle to get his men back safely from the *Endurance* fiasco. These events were traumatic and forced him to dig deep into his spiritual and physical reserves. Had Shackleton been the icon that management gurus wish to make him he would have been a great deal less a man and a great deal less interesting.

His diary entry for 9 January 1909 – the farthest South entry – reads in part: '... the icy gale cut us to the bone, we looked south with our powerful glasses, but could see nothing but the dead white snow plain. There was no break in the plateau as it extended towards the Pole, and we feel sure that the goal we have failed to reach lies on this plain ... Homeward bound at last. Whatever regrets may be, we have done our best.' The realism and the philosophy of the man are there, understated but patent – disappointment, determination, survival.

The Royal Geographical Society and the Admiralty were the corporate sectors of Shackleton's time, against which he fought for the right of individuals, he and his comrades. He led by example. There was an expectation, an unspoken demand, that those same comrades give as much as they could. For those who didn't, he had little sympathy.

The truth about Shackleton is that he was human, not super-human. His dreams did not come true, he was not the person he would like to have been. For most of his life he carried the expectations of and responsibility for his parents, sisters and wayward brother. He was an outsider and, as he grew older, on the periphery of the lives of his wife and children. His restlessness never allowed him to find peace with himself. He loved life and he lived it to the last breath he drew, but his romantic spirit was never satisfied.

Only in death did he find the peace he searched for and the recognition that was fleeting in his lifetime. And only in death did he reach that place that always just eluded his grasp, where no further demands could be made on his energy and vision.

Speaking in Sydney in March 1917, he gave what might well serve as his epitaph:

> *'Death is a very little thing – the smallest thing in the world. I can tell you that, for I have come face to face with death ... I know that death scarcely weighs in the scale against a man's appointed task. Perhaps in the quiet hours of night, when you think over the things I have said, you will feel the little snakes of doubt twisting in your heart. I have known them. Put them aside. If we have to die, we will die in the pride of manhood, our eyes on the goal and our hearts beating time to the instinct within us.'*

Above: Eleanor Shackleton (1879-1960) at her birthplace Kilkea House in 1958. She described how she and her other brothers and sisters were born in the front room upstairs. (Courtesy Richard Greene) Centre: Edward Arthur Alexander, Baron Shackleton of Burley KG, PC, OBE, FRS (1911-94) in 1988. Younger son of Ernest Shackleton; distinguished parliamentarian in the Commons and the Lords, where he became Labour Leader of the House; explorer, writer, businessman, President of the Royal Geographical Society, with long-standing interests in science and the South Atlantic, especially the Falklands. Right: Dr Jan Piggott, Keeper of Archives at Dulwich College; in 2000 he organized a remarkable exhibition on Shackleton at Dulwich, editing Shackleton, The Antarctic and Endurance *to accompany the exhibition. (Courtesy Judith Faulkner) Hon. Alexandra Shackleton only daughter of Lord Shackleton; President of the James Caird Society who has done much to promote the memory of her grandfather. Harding Dunnett (1909-2000), lifelong devotee of Sir Ernest Shackleton, both of whom were past pupils of Dulwich College; founder and chairman of the James Caird Society.*

At the opening of the exhibition The Endurance. Shackleton's Legendary Antarctic Expedition, *Peabody Essex Museum, Salem, Massachusetts, June 2000 – left to right: Conrad Anker, Californian mountaineer, participant in* Shackleton's Antarctic Adventure *IMAX film; Jonathan Shackleton; Caroline Alexander, whose book,* Mrs Chippy's Last Expedition (1997), *led to the publication in 1998 of her* The Endurance. Shackleton's Legendary Antarctic Expedition *to accompany the remarkable Shackleton exhibition at the American Museum of Natural History in New York in 1999. This started a wave of worldwide interest in Shackleton.*

Bibliography & Recommended Reading

ALEXANDER, Caroline, *Mrs Chippy's Last Expedition: The Remarkable Journal of Shackleton's Polar-Bound Cat* (HarperCollins, New York, 1997).

——, *The* Endurance. *Shackleton's Legendary Expedition* (Bloomsbury, London 1998). Excellent selection of well reproduced Hurley photos and good text.

AMUNDSEN, Roald, *My Life as an Explorer* (New York 1928).

BARRINGTON, Amy, *The Barringtons* (Ponsonby and Gibbs, Dublin 1917).

BEGBIE, Harold, *Shackleton – A Memory* (Mills & Boon, London 1922).

BICKELL, Lennard, *Shackleton's Forgotten Argonauts* (Macmillan, Australia 1982). Account of often-overlooked Ross Sea Party of Shackleton's Imperial Trans-Antarctic Expedition.

CROSSLEY, Louise, *Explore Antarctica* (Cambridge University Press 1995). Good slim introduction to Antarctica.

DUNNETT, Harding, *Shackleton's Boat* (Neville and Harding 1996). Complete history of the *James Caird* by Shackleton expert who was at Dulwich College when Shackleton was on his *Quest* expedition.

FISHER, Margery and James, *Shackleton* (James Barrie, London 1957). Sensible, well-documented biography of Shackleton, completed when a number of his crewmen were still alive.

GWYNN, Stephen, *Captain Scott* (John Lane, London 1929).

HARTWIG, G., *The Polar World* (Longmans, Green, & Co.,London 1874).

HEACOK, Kim, *Shackleton. The Antartic Challenge* (National Geographic, New York 1999).

HEADLAND, Robert, *Chronological List of Antarctic Expeditions and Related Events* (Cambridge University Press 1989). Mine of carefully documented information; new edition expected soon.

HUNTFORD, Roland, *Scott and Amundsen* (Hodder and Stoughton, London 1979). Pro-Amundsen and anti-Scott.

——, *Shackleton* (Hodder and Stoughton, London 1985). Comprehensive biography written by an admirer.

HURLEY, Frank, *South with* Endurance. *The Photographs of Frank Hurley* (Bloomsbury, London 2001). Definitive collection of Hurley's *Endurance* photographs with contributions on the man, the photographs and the photographer.

HUSSEY, Leonard, *South with Shackleton* (Samson Low, London 1949). Interesting reflections on the 'Boss' by the only crew member at Shackleton's burial.

LANSING, Alfred, Endurance, *Shackleton's Incredible Voyage* (Hodder and Stoughton, London 1959). Great account of this extraordinary journey, widely read in the USA.

LOCKE, Stephen, *George Marston: Shackleton's Antarctic Artist* (Hampshire County Council 2000).

LYNCH, Wayne, *Penguins of the World* (Firefly Books, Canada 1997).

MARKHAM, Albert, *The Life of Sir Clements R. Markham* (John Murray, London 1917).

MILL, Hugh Robert, *The Life of Sir Ernest Shackleton* (Heinemann, London 1923). First biography written in close consultation with Shackleton's family.

MILLS, Leif, *Frank Wild* (Caedmon of Whitby, North Yorkshire 1999). Useful life of Shackleton's most doughty travelling companion, who also went south with Scott and Mawson.

MORRELL, Margot and Stephanie CAPPARELL, *Shackleton's Way. Leadership lessons from the Great Antarctic Explorer* (Viking, New York 2001). Good analysis from modern business viewpoint of what made Shackleton such an outstanding leader.

NEWMAN, Stanley (ed.), *Shackleton's Lieutenant* (Polar Publications, Aukland 1990). *Nimrod* diary of Aeneas Mackintosh.

PIGGOTT, Jan. *Shackleton. The* Antarctic *and* Endurance (Dulwich College 2000). Five essays by experts, and a superbly produced catalogue for an exhibition about Shackleton.

READER'S DIGEST. *Great Stories from the Frozen Continent* (New York 1998). Useful reference book.

RICHARDS, Richard. *The Ross Sea Shore Party 1914-1917.* (Scott Polar Research Institute, Cambridge 1962). Valuable as one of only two first-hand accounts of this part of the Imperial Trans-Antarctic Expedition.

ROSOVE, Michael, *Antarctica 1772-1922. Freestanding Publications through 1999*; (Adelie Books, California 2001). Excellent new bibliography and standard reference work.

RUBIN, Jeff, *Antarctica* (Lonely Planet Guide, Melbourne 2000). Useful guide for the visitor to Antarctica.

SCOTT, Robert F., *The Voyage of the 'Discovery'* (John Murray, London 1905).

—— (ed.), *The South Polar Times,* Volume 1 (London 1907).

SHACKLETON, Ernest, *The Heart of the Antarctic* (Heinemann, London 1909). Shackleton's own account of the 1907-1909 *Nimrod* expedition.

——, *South* (Heinemann, London 1919). Shackleton's own account of his *Endurance* expedition.

SHACKLETON, Jonathan. *The Shackletons of Ballitore [1580-1987]* (Private, 1988). Brief history of Irish branch of the family, with genealogical sheets.

SMITH, Michael, *An Unsung Hero – Tom Crean* (Collins, Cork 2000). Great tribute to a remarkable man, from his humble beginnings in County Kerry. Served with Scott and Shackleton.

SOPER, Tony, *Antarctica – A guide to the Wildlife* (Bradt Travel Guides, Bucks UK 2000). Best pocket guide to Antarctic wildlife, illustrated by Captain Scott's granddaughter.

SPUFFORD, Francis, *I May Be Some Time* (Faber & Faber, London 1996). Philosophical essay about British obsession with frozen places.

THOMSON, John, *Shackleton's Captain – A Biography of Frank Worsley* (Mosaic Press, Toronto 1999).

WILD, Frank, *Shackleton's Last Voyage. The Story of the* Quest (Cassell, London 1923).

WILSON, David and ELDER, D.B., *Cheltenham in Antarctica* (Reardon, Cheltenham 2000). Biography of David's great uncle Edward (Ted) Wilson. Good information and illustrations.

WORSLEY, Frank, *Shackleton's Boat Journey* (Hodder and Stoughton, London 1933). Excellent account by navigator of the *James Caird.*

Recommended websites

www.antarctic-circle.org   www.ernestshackleton.net   www.jamescairdsociety.com   www.70south.com

Acknowledgments

Jonathan and John have been assisted by many experts and institutions. We especially thank the following:

In travels to Antarctica: Tony Soper and Anna Sutcliffe, Geoff Green and Angela Holmes, and Dave Burkitt at Port Lockroy.

In Ireland: Richard and Claudia Greene, Kevin Hannafin, Kevin Kenny, Noel Lambe, Brendan O'Brien and the Crean family, Joe O'Farrell, Frank and Seamus Taaffe, Margaret O'Riordan at the Athy Heritage Centre, and the late Richard and Mary Shackleton.

In the United Kingdom: Robert Headland, Archivist and Curator, Lucy Martin and Phillipa Smith her predecessor as Photographic Library Manager at the Scott Polar Research Institute, Cambridge, for the use of their archives; Daphne Knott and her colleagues at the National Maritime Museum, London; Andrew Tathum and Sarah Strong at the Royal Geographical Society, London, for the use of their archives; Valerie Mattingley of National Geographic Society UK; Tom Lamb of Christie's, London; John Blackborow, Bob Burton, Rod Downie (BAS), Wendy Driver, the late Harding Dunnett, David Harding, Dr Jan Piggott at Dulwich College, Roger Putt, Hon. Alexandra Shackleton, John and Sally Sparks, David Wilson, and many others.

In the United States: Charles and Miranda Shackleton, Regina Daly and Rob Stephenson.

Illustration Credits

Amundsen family 54; Athy Heritage Centre 26, 93; Barrington (1917) 13, 14, 15; Bernacchi (1938) 59; Canterbury Museum, Christchurch 106; Central Navy Museum, Leningrad 50; Christie's Images, London 108; Connolly, T. 158; Cornford, T. 44; Governors of Dulwich College 31; Eliot, D. 106; Greenhow, D. 13; Greene, Richard 202; Gwynn (1929) 58; Hartwig (1874) 46, 47, 52; Larken, E. 72; *Lyttelton Times* 107; Markham (1917) 57; McEwan, R. 84; Mill, H.R. 28, 33, 36, 82; National Geographic Society, Washington DC, endpapers; National Maritime Museum, London 43, 53, 95; private collection 67, 198; Roberts Library, University of Toronto 131; Scott (1907) 76; Scott Polar Research Institute 40, 76, 102, 103, 115, 116, 143, 145, 146, 147, 150, 151, 152, 157, 174, 181, 184, 185, 186, 187, 189, 192, 193, 194, 195, 198, 199; Scottish Royal Geographical Society 51; Shackleton family 12, 17, 19, 20, 22, 27, 28, 38, 46, 48, 53, 81, 88, 112, 133, 140, 160, 172, 177, 202, 203; Shackleton (1909) 98, 104, 111, 113, 119, 127, 129; Shackleton (1919) 165; Wellington National Art Gallery 49; White, J. 19.

Index

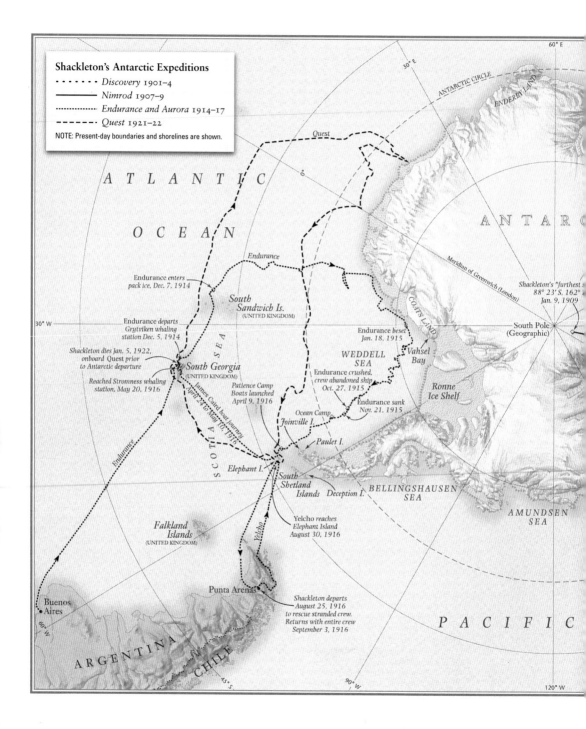

Shackleton's Antarctic Expeditions

· · · · · · Discovery 1901–4
———— Nimrod 1907–9
················ Endurance and Aurora 1914–17
– – – – Quest 1921–22

NOTE: Present-day boundaries and shorelines are shown.

ATLANTIC

OCEAN

ANTARC

ANTARCTIC CIRCLE

ENDERBY LAND

60° E

30° E

Quest

0°

Endurance

Endurance *enters*
pack ice, Dec. 7, 1914

Endurance *departs*
Grytviken whaling
station Dec. 5, 1914

Shackleton dies Jan. 5, 1922,
onboard Quest prior
to Antarctic departure

Reached Stromness whaling
station, May 20, 1916

South Georgia
(UNITED KINGDOM)

James Caird boat journey
April 24 to May 10, 1916

Patience Camp
Boats launched
April 9, 1916

Ocean Camp

Joinville I.

Paulet I.

Elephant I.

South
Shetland
Islands Deception I.

Yelcho reaches
Elephant Island
August 30, 1916

Falkland
Islands
(UNITED KINGDOM)

Yelcho

Buenos
Aires

60° W

Punta Arenas

Shackleton departs
August 25, 1916.
Returns with entire crew
September 3, 1916

ARGENTINA

CHILE

45° S

90° W

South
Sandwich Is.
(UNITED KINGDOM)

S C O T I A   S E A

Endurance

Meridian of Greenwich (London)

COATS LAND

Shackleton's "furthest s
88° 23' S, 162°
Jan. 9, 1909

South Pole
(Geographic)

Endurance beset
Jan. 18, 1915

WEDDELL
SEA

Vahsel
Bay

Endurance crushed,
crew abandoned ship
Oct. 27, 1915

Endurance sank
Nov. 21, 1915

Ronne
Ice Shelf

BELLINGSHAUSEN
SEA

AMUNDSEN
SEA

PACIFIC

120° W

30° W

60° E

Endurance